# SAVED AT THE SEAWALL

# SAVED AT THE SEAWALL

## Stories from the September 11 Boat Lift

## JESSICA DuLONG

### FOREWORD BY
### MITCHELL ZUCKOFF

THREE HILLS

AN IMPRINT OF

CORNELL UNIVERSITY PRESS

ITHACA AND LONDON

First published in 2017 as *Dust to Deliverance: Untold Stories from the Maritime
Evacuation on September 11* by McGraw Hill Education

*Dust to Deliverance: Untold Stories from the Maritime Evacuation on
September 11* was funded in part by Furthermore grants in publishing,
a program of the J.M. Kaplan Fund.

First published in paperback 2021 by Cornell University Press


Library of Congress Cataloging-in-Publication Data

Names: DuLong, Jessica, author.
Title: Saved at the seawall: stories from the September 11 boat lift /
   Jessica DuLong; foreword by Mitchell Zuckoff.
Other titles: Dust to deliverance
Description: Ithaca [New York]: Three Hills, an imprint of
   Cornell University Press, 2021. | First published in 2017 by
   McGraw Hill Education under title: Dust to deliverance:
   untold stories from the maritime evacuation on September 11. |
   Includes bibliographical references and index.
Identifiers: LCCN 2020058212 (print) | LCCN 2020058213 (ebook) |
   ISBN 9781501759123 (paperback) | ISBN 9781501759130 (pdf) |
   ISBN 9781501759147 (epub)
Subjects: LCSH: September 11 Terrorist Attacks, 2001. |
   Evacuation of civilians—New York (State)—New York. |
   Emergency management—New York (State)—New York. |
   Rescues—New York (State)—New York.
Classification: LCC HV6432.7.D855 2021 (print) |
   LCC HV6432.7 (ebook) | DDC 974.7/1044—dc23
LC record available at https://lccn.loc.gov/2020058212
LC ebook record available at https://lccn.loc.gov/2020058213

Photos used with permission of the New York City Police
Department copyright © 2001.

To my parents, Peter and Gretchen,
whose lessons about language and
goodness charted my course


To Ben, Zillin, and Jude,
for buoying me with love and laughter

# Contents

| | | |
|---|---|---:|
| *Foreword* | | IX |
| *Preface to the Paperback Edition* | | XIII |
| *September 11, 2001, Timeline* | | XVII |

**PART ONE**    **The Situation**

| | | |
|---|---|---:|
| CHAPTER 1: | *"It was a jet. It was a jet. It was a jet."* | 3 |
| CHAPTER 2: | *"Shut it down! Shut it down!"* | 22 |
| CHAPTER 3: | *"NEW YORK CITY CLOSED TO ALL TRAFFIC"* | 41 |

**PART TWO**    **The Evacuation**

| | | |
|---|---|---:|
| CHAPTER 4: | *"I was gonna swim to Jersey."* | 54 |
| CHAPTER 5: | *"It was like breathing dirt."* | 71 |
| CHAPTER 6: | *"We're in the water!"* | 86 |
| CHAPTER 7: | *"Gray ghosts"* | 97 |
| CHAPTER 8: | *"A sea of boats"* | 114 |
| CHAPTER 9: | *"I need a boat."* | 134 |

**PART THREE**    **The Aftermath**

| | | |
|---|---|---:|
| CHAPTER 10: | *"We have to tell us what to do."* | 160 |
| CHAPTER 11: | *"Sell first, repent later."* | 178 |
| CHAPTER 12: | *"Okay, I am in charge."* | 191 |
| CHAPTER 13: | *"They'd do it again tomorrow."* | 199 |
| CHAPTER 14: | *September 11, 2016* | 208 |

| | |
|---|---:|
| *Epilogue* | 218 |
| *Acknowledgments* | 220 |
| *Vessel Participants* | 222 |
| *Notes* | 225 |
| *Index* | 231 |

# FOREWORD

NOT LONG AGO I received a message from a tugboat crew member who had witnessed the events of 9/11 from the waters around Lower Manhattan. He had taken video from his boat of the burning twin towers of the World Trade Center that recorded the last moments of victims who fell or leapt to their deaths. As he filmed, he spontaneously narrated the horrors, using salty language and a tone that, in retrospect, didn't fit the enormity of the events. His sense that his comments were disrespectful haunted him and he never shared his footage publicly, even though he knew that the recording would be a valuable addition to the historical record.

The passage of time, like flowing water, creates a channel through even the hardest stone. When he contacted me, the mariner said the years had revised his thinking: "Now I know it's more important for everyone to see and know what happened that day, versus some comments I made," he wrote in an email. I viewed a copy of his video then connected him with archivists at the National September 11 Memorial & Museum in New York who gratefully included it in their unparalleled collection.

That story came to mind as I read Jessica DuLong's remarkable book *Saved at the Seawall*, which filled a large gap in my own knowledge and research. Her work has brought to the surface long-overlooked tales of heroism and sacrifice, recounting the actions and sharing the character of a community response to tragedy as immediate and impressive as any in history.

Major facts about September 11, 2001, are well established: 19 terrorists acting on behalf of Al Qaeda and Osama bin Laden hijacked four commercial passenger jets and turned them into guided missiles aimed at government and civilian targets, killing nearly 3,000 people in New York City, Shanksville, and Washington D.C. Those murders reshaped the world, and we are still coming to understand this new political, economic, social, and diplomatic terrain. It is for good reason, then, that 9/11 is among the most exhaustively examined moments of the past century. And yet, 20 years later, essential, insightful, and unique perspectives are still coming to light—and deservedly so.

All of us who write about 9/11 are indebted to the *New York Times* for, among other reasons, the newspaper's "Portraits of Grief" project. In brief vignettes, gifted reporters and writers memorialized and humanized the victims. Their work began almost immediately after the fall of the towers, the fires at the Pentagon were extinguished, and recovery began in the field where United Airlines Flight 93 crash-landed, and it continued for years. The *Times* reporters told the stories of the dead in 2001 and then followed up with accounts that revealed how those left behind were coping, or not. By taking such an intimate approach to attacks of enormous scale and complexity, the newspaper declared that every individual loss deserved thoughtful, sustained attention and that every perspective and experience of 9/11 merited deep reflection.

Which brings me back to DuLong, who has extended the project begun by "Portraits in Grief" by listening to and then presenting the words of individuals who suffered and persevered on that bright September day and then long afterward. In this gripping narrative, if readers will forgive the expression, DuLong has gone into uncharted waters of recorded history.

Overwhelmingly, the study of 9/11 has focused on what happened in the air and on the ground. Entire books have been written about Flight 93, whose 40 passengers and crew members fought back against the hijackers and brought down the plane well short of its intended target in Washington, D.C. Other books have examined the military response, or the Pentagon fire, or the fall of the twin towers. Many have told the tale of a single survivor, hero, or victim. The same ground-and-air focus characterizes my work, first covering the attacks as a reporter for the *Boston Globe* and then writing a book-length narrative about 9/11.

By taking to the water, a fitting decision considering her own rich history on the Hudson River, DuLong has applied her hard-earned maritime knowledge in the name of honoring the men and women who answered the ancient code that compels mariners to proceed with all speed to a distress call. Like firefighters, the captains and crews who took part in the 9/11 boat lift moved toward danger, putting themselves in peril, to save others. Their obligation wasn't legal but moral.

DuLong knows why these roughly 800 mariners aboard at least 150 watercraft in New York Harbor answered the call, and now we can, too.

Mitchell Zuckoff, author of
*Fall and Rise: The Story of 9/11*

PREFACE TO THE PAPERBACK EDITION

MOMENTS THAT DEFINE endings also mark beginnings. On September 11, 2001, history split into *before* and *after*. This rift occurred in an instant, at 8:46 that morning. Then the horror unspooled for hours, days, weeks, and even years as the toll of death, destruction, and, later, disease continued to rise. Life was irrevocably altered.

Two decades later, our world has once more been rent in two. Instead of mourning nearly 3,000 murdered on a single morning, we grieve the millions of people killed by COVID-19 worldwide. This time, the division between *before* and *after* came not as a sudden shock of violence but over the course of months as outbreaks spread across the globe. Even here in New York City, a world epicenter, some neighborhoods suffered relatively few deaths or disruptions while others have shouldered terrible losses. Yet, the pandemic has forced all of us, regardless of nation, state, or zip code, to confront profound changes. And none of us knows yet what to expect in what Don DeLillo described in *Falling Man* as "the days after."

Ruptures caused by historic events like terrorist attacks and pandemics leave us reeling, struggling to grasp what it means to survive—to remake our lives in the aftermath. Over time I've come to believe that our best hope arises out of respecting our scars as evidence of our ability to persevere—to build a future out of our past. Every scar has a story. In the wake of trauma, these stories help us make meaning out of suffering, supporting our efforts to reassemble the pieces of our lives in the permanently altered *after*.

On Friday, September 14, 2001, I didn't yet understand any of this. After four days supplying Hudson River water to fight fires at the World Trade Center, retired New York City fireboat *John J. Harvey* docked at her home berth on Manhattan's western shore. I was part of the crew preparing to return to the regular world—or whatever new version of it would greet us outside the perimeter of destruction.

After securing lines, the boat's chief engineer, Tim Ivory, jumped the gap from the 1931 vessel's caprail to Pier 63 Maritime. A crowd circled up around him—friends of the boat, regulars on the pier, others I didn't recognize—all hungry for information about what was happening down there. Their questions prompted answers, then a torrent of stories.

I watched through the wheelhouse windows as Tim held court. My own words had fled. I feared that confining this time, these events within words would dull the sharp-edged truths, boxing them in, leaving them muted and pruned at the edges by the limits of lexicon. No language felt sufficient.

Over the coming months, as people from every corner chimed in to give their accounts of that day, the fireboat offered me respite. Relieved of official duties, the boat returned to her retiree status and, once the harbor reopened to nonessential traffic, again started taking people out on cruises. In my spot below decks at the control pedestal, swinging the levers that power the boat's propellers, the roar of engines drowned out all the talk. But, of course, this defining moment—the deadliest hostile attack on United States soil—could not go unvoiced forever.

Only after years of avoiding conversation about my time at Ground Zero did I finally make my peace with the human need for September 11 stories. Chronicling catastrophe necessarily creates a distance, a remove. I could hear this distance when I compared the tight, pinched cadences of first responders taped in the days immediately after the attacks with the interviews of those same people I recorded years later. Ultimately, creating that emotional space is necessary for forging a path forward. In time, I recognized that the importance of preserving this history outweighed my need to fend off the anguish of these accounts—both others' and my own.

Understanding the reluctance some survivors and rescuers felt about delving into their own harrowing memories made me all the more grateful to the many who did agree to interviews— particularly those who shared for the first time their full stories, with all the raw details. They agreed to do so for the sake of documenting this pivotal moment in history, and that willingness brought this book to life.

Reading their stories now, under the weight of the pandemic and all its devastating repercussions, provides a window into what's possible. On these pages we see the collaboration, comity, and community that offer a promise of who we can be, both now and *after*.

On September 11, and in the days and weeks that followed, people here in New York City came together. We gathered en masse at makeshift memorials in Union Square, outside the city's firehouses, and along the border of the "frozen zone." We lit candles, posted signs, shed tears, and stood together with strangers in solemn silence.

In March 2020, instead of togetherness, COVID compelled isolation, calling upon us to wear a mask, wash our hands, and maintain six-plus feet of distance. We steered clear of others— sanitizing our groceries, quarantining our mail, and fearing our neighbors. However collective our trauma, our individual family tragedies have taken place in quarantine—in homes and hospitals—rendering the uptick in numbers largely faceless to those on the outside. Owing to pandemic restrictions, a grieving nation has been unable to properly mourn its dead.

How will we ever recover?

We will, as we always have, through drawing upon the best of humanity that rises up in the bleakest times. What saves us is recognizing our place in the long arc of history. What saves us are stories that forge human connections across divides. What saves us, finally, is hope.

In *Hope in the Dark*—a book I've taken to carrying around with me as an antidote to the grinding miseries of 2020—Rebecca Solnit writes: "Hope locates itself in the premises that we don't know what will happen and that, in the spaciousness of uncertainty, you recognize that you may be able to influence the outcomes—you alone or you in concert with a few dozen or several million others." In this dire moment, hopelessness, like helplessness, is not an option.

We have much to learn from the mariners and others who, when the planes struck, stepped out of their workaday roles to become first responders. Over and over again they chose to help. They recognized fellow humans in peril and did all they could to come to their aid. Each of us has this capacity within. What choices can we make today to act out our hope, our humanity? How can we connect with others by listening, really listening, to their stories?

In this time unlike any we have known, the story of the largest boat lift in history serves as a vital reminder of the reflexive resourcefulness and resounding human goodness that light up the darkest days.

Jessica DuLong
Brooklyn, New York
February 2021

# September 11, 2001, Timeline

## A.M.

| | |
|---|---|
| 8:46:40 | American Airlines Flight 11 crashes into 1 World Trade Center (the North Tower) |
| 08:47 | MTA subway operator alerts MTA Subway Control Center of an explosion in the WTC and begins emergency procedures |
| 08:52 | PATH trains begin emergency procedures and proceed to evacuate WTC station and return Manhattan-bound trains to New Jersey |
| 09:02:59 | United Airlines Flight 175 crashes into 2 World Trade Center (the South Tower) |
| 09:10 | U.S. Coast Guard closes Port of New York and New Jersey Port Authority of NY and NJ closes all its bridges and tunnels |
| 09:17 | FAA shuts down all NYC airports |
| 09:37:45 | American Airlines Flight 77 hits the west wall of the Pentagon |
| 09:58:59 | South Tower collapses |
| 10:03:11 | United Airlines Flight 93 crashes in Pennsylvania |
| 10:20 | NYC Transit suspends all subway service |
| 10:28:22 | North Tower collapses |
| 10:30 | NJ Transit stops rail service into Manhattan's Penn Station |
| 10:45 | U.S. Coast Guard calls for "all available boats" to assist evacuation of Lower Manhattan; PATH operations suspended |
| 11:02 | Mayor Giuliani calls for evacuation south of Canal Street |

## P.M.

| | |
|---|---|
| 05:20 | 7 World Trade Center, headquarters of NYC Office of Emergency Management, collapses |

*Sources:*

U.S. Department of Transportation's John A. Volpe National Transportation Systems Center, "Effects of Catastrophic Events on Transportation System Management and Operations: New York City—September 11," 2/6/17, https://ntl.bts.gov/lib/jpodocs/repts_te/14129.htm.

U.S. Department of Commerce, Technology Administration, National Institute of Standards and Technology, "Final report on the collapse of the World Trade Center towers," 4/26/17, http://ws680.nist.gov/publication/get_pdf.cfm?pub_id=909017.

P.J. Capelotti, Rogue Wave: The U.S. Coast Guard on and after 9/11, Washington, DC, U.S. Coast Guard Historians Office, 4/27/17, https://www.uscg.mil/history/91101/pubs/911_Rogue_Wave.pdf.

1 Port Imperial
2 Intrepid Sea, Air, and Space Museum (Pier 84)
3 Piers 81–83
4 Jacob K. Javits Convention Center
5 Lincoln Harbor
6 Pier 63
7 Pier 62
8 Pier 61
9 Pier 60
10 Pier 59
11 Pier 53
12 Long Slip
13 Pier 40
14 Downtown Boathouse (Pier 26)
15 PATH Tubes (Formerly H&M Hudson Tubes)
16 Paulus Hook
17 Colgate Clock
18 Morris Canal
19 Liberty Landing Marina
20 Liberty State Park
21 Red Hook Container Terminal
22 South Street Seaport
23 Brooklyn Navy Yard
24 North Cove
25 Whitehall Terminal (Staten Island Ferry)
26 World Trade Center complex
27 1 World Trade Center (Tower One) (North Tower)
28 2 World Trade Center (Tower Two) (South Tower)
29 3 World Trade Center
30 4 World Trade Center
31 5 World Trade Center (Borders Books and Music)
32 6 World Trade Center
33 7 World Trade Center
34 1 World Financial Center
35 2 World Financial Center
36 3 World Financial Center
37 4 World Financial Center
38 Winter Garden
39 World Financial Center Terminal
40 North Pedestrian Bridge
41 South Pedestrian Bridge
42 Gateway Plaza (VIP Yacht Cruises offices and St. Joseph's Chapel on the first floor)
43 Albany Street townhouse
44 Zuccotti Park
45 New York Stock Exchange
46 South Cove
47 Robert F. Wagner Jr. Park
48 Pier A
49 The Battery
50 Battery Park
51 U.S. Coast Guard offices
52 Downtown Heliport
53 Pier 11

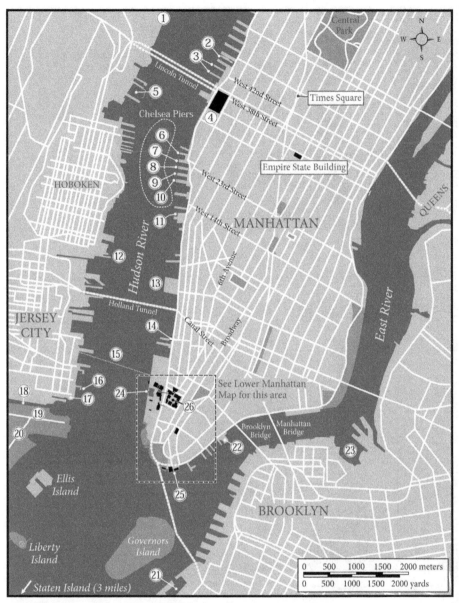

New York Harbor. Map by Mike Bechthold.

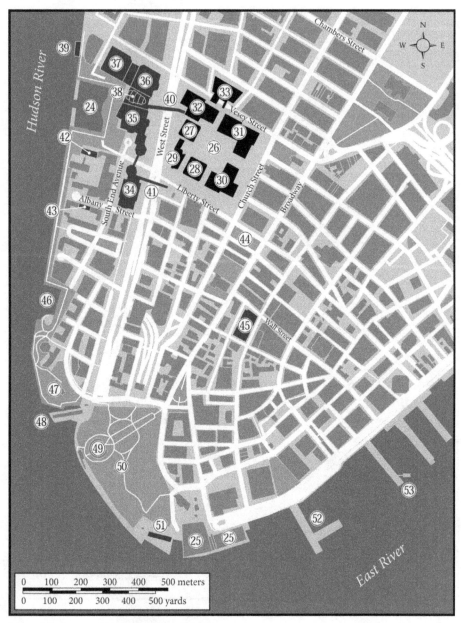

Lower Manhattan. Map by Mike Bechthold.

# PART ONE

———⊸∞∞⊸———

# THE SITUATION

It is at night that faith in light is admirable.
—Edmond Rostand, *Chantecler*

CHAPTER 1

# "It was a jet. It was a jet. It was a jet."

As the sun tracks across the sky on this overcast, 78-degree morning, the clouds part ways leaving behind a mazarine blue. There is no dust. No smoke. The heaviness in today's air is only the humidity of late summer. A forest of sailboat masts bobs in the rectangular notch of Manhattan's North Cove. The propeller wash from New York Waterway and Liberty Landing ferries dropping off and picking up passengers at the new World Financial Center terminal, 150 paces or so to the north of the small harbor, pushes little waves through the 75-foot gap in the breakwater. *Mis Moondance*, a 66-foot charter yacht, motors in and maneuvers into a slip among the wooden floating docks. A blue and white police boat holds station just outside the cove's entrance, blue light flashing above the pilothouse.

To a casual observer, unaware of the date, it might be hard to say if this quiet is just the regular hush of Sunday or something more solemn. Certainly the pedestrian plaza is far less populated on Sundays than it would be on a weekday morning—a Tuesday morning, say. Surely all the street closures and police barricades thwarting access have kept some people away, while reminding any who might have momentarily forgotten that this is no ordinary day.

Several blocks inland, beneath the trees in the National September 11 Memorial plaza, the fifteenth anniversary commemoration has begun. About 8,000 people have assembled for this year's annual ritual. Families of those lost will read, 30 at a time, the names of the 2,977 people who died from injuries or expo-sures sustained 15 years ago today, plus the six killed in the bomb-ing of the World Trade Center on February 26, 1993.

At 8:46 A.M., bells ring in the plaza and across New York City to announce the first of six moments of silence. This one marks the moment when American Airlines Flight 11 ripped through the northern facade of the World Trade Center's North Tower between the ninety-third and ninety-ninth floors. By the water's edge, the chuff-chuff-chuff of a helicopter hovering over the Hud-son never lets up. Silence on the waterfront is merely theoretical.

Sunday joggers, earbuds in, digital music players strapped around biceps, continue on their morning runs. Bicyclists keep biking, tourists snap photographs, parents herd young children. But two New York Waterway ferries pause, foregoing their usual over and back, over and back, to linger in reverence. Above them glints the new 1 World Trade Center, the base of its spire reflected in an adjacent skyscraper, also new. Between them stands a third tower, still under construction, the outstretched arm of a crane loitering above its uppermost reaches—a skeleton waiting for workers to finish grafting on its reflective skin.

When the bell chimes again at 9:03 A.M., the moment that United Airlines Flight 175 crashed into the South Tower's south-ern facade between the seventy-seventh and eighty-fifth floors, a lone gentleman with close-cropped gray hair is sitting silently before the cross inside St. Joseph's Chapel where a special anni-versary mass is scheduled to commence at 10 A.M., one minute after the South Tower fell, and 28 minutes before the North Tower followed it to the ground.

The day after the attacks, this chapel was converted into a makeshift, volunteer-run supply house for distributing donated goods. Rescue workers turned its plate glass windows into a mes-sage board of sorts, tracing pleas, prayers, and pronouncements into the gray dust: "Revenge is sweet." "Goodness will prevail." "It doesn't matter how you died, it only matters where you go." "You woke a sleeping giant." Among the scrawls was the word "*Invictus*." Latin for *unconquerable*, it's the title of an 1875 poem by William Ernest Henley that begins:

"Out of the night that covers me,
Black as the Pit from pole to pole,
I thank whatever gods may be
For my unconquerable soul."

Other messages, more practical than poetic, included: "Go to Stuyvesant High School to sleep" and "Lt. John Crisci call home."

I first transcribed these missives into a small reporter's notebook while standing in the dust of September 12, 2001. Although I wasn't technically reporting at the time, a writer's lifelong habits run deep. I scribbled down the words in an attempt to collect the details that I hoped might somehow help me make sense of the unfathomable ruination at hand. At 28 years old, I was still a newcomer to New York City, having moved here in January of 2000. By the following September, I was just six months into the hands-on apprenticeship that had launched my new career as a marine engineer. I was a novice in every sense of the word.

Now, a decade and a half later, I've risen from assistant engineer to chief, a "hawsepiper" who's come up through the ranks (climbing, metaphorically, up the anchor chain through an opening in the bow called the hawsepipe) by learning on the job rather than in school. New York harbor's maritime community is my community.

After 15 years in the industry, my view of everything has changed. Now, on this overcast Tuesday morning, when I notice the dull red paint coating one section of the curved steel railing along the water's edge, I recognize it as primer, evidence of a painting project in process. This is the railing that I climbed over, on September 12, as I bolted from threats of a fourth building collapse, scrambling to board the boat that had so recently become my workplace: retired 1931 New York City fireboat *John J. Harvey*. No longer an active-duty vessel with the Fire Department of the City of New York (FDNY), the boat had been operating as a preservation project and living museum when it was called back into service to help fight New York City's most devastating fires.

# CHAPTER 5

# *"It was like breathing dirt."*

TO PROTECT HIMSELF FROM THE DEBRIS STILL FALLING after the South Tower's collapse, volunteer firefighter Nussberger climbed through the entrance of a domed office building with blown-out windows and a green marble lobby strewn with ashy wreckage. Once sheltered, he struggled to piece together the details. That thump he'd heard in the split second before the world went silent and still, when the air had suddenly become too thick, too solid to transmit the vibrations that humans perceive as sound—just before the wave of agony that later roused him— was the impact of his body being flung against the side of this building, 2 World Financial Center, 70 feet away from where he'd last stood.

At some point Nussberger made his way out of the rubble-filled building and wandered back outside. He began stumbling across the waterfront plaza, struggling to breathe. *I'm gonna have a heart attack. I know I'm gonna have a heart attack.* He was fading in and out of coherence—crawling, walking, and falling again as he crossed an outdoor plaza until eventually he found his way down a ramp to the Hudson River. He collapsed again on the hexagonal paving stones along the water's edge. This time he couldn't get up. The adrenaline that had carried him thus far seemed to have quit.

Against the seawall in front of him, a fireboat loaded with evacuees was preparing to pull out. Some men gathered on the shoreline spotted Nussberger collapsed in the dust in his turnout gear. They heaved him over the railing and onto the boat below, one gripping his arm so hard that it left a full handprint bruised into his skin. Two men helped him to the bow where he lay down atop a pile of fire hose. Disoriented by pain, Nussberger looked up at the huge bow pipe above him and tried to piece together where on earth he could have ended up.

———— ⊶⊷ ————

A short time earlier Richard Larrabee, commerce director for the Port Authority of New York and New Jersey, had wondered the same thing. He had been standing in the lobby of the Marriott Hotel. Now he was crawling through wreckage on his hands and knees. When light finally penetrated the darkness he looked up and saw a street lamp. *Where the hell is there a traffic light inside the World Trade Center?*

Then it dawned on him that he was outside. He had wound up on West Street. Somehow, he had been spared when the hotel that sat sandwiched between the two trade center towers was cleaved from top to bottom "as if a giant scissors had snipped the building in two," as reporters would later describe it. While reinforced beams installed following the 1993 bombing had protected one half of the lobby, the other half was crushed, taking whole fire companies—at least 40 firefighters—along with it.

All morning the Marriott Hotel had served as a critical escape route allowing close to a thousand people fleeing 1 World Trade Center to leave without facing the danger of walking outside. Since the first minutes of the disaster, hotel staffers had been ushering people to safety. They'd also helped redirect firefighters and police officers who, unfamiliar with the layout of the trade center complex, had chosen the most visible entrance.

By the time Larrabee arrived, just before ten o'clock, the flow of evacuees had slowed. The lobby was a blur of black turnout gear as the sea of helmeted firefighters who'd assembled awaited orders. Sirens wailed. The apprehension was palpable. Still, the hotel had seemed a safe enough distance away from the fires for Larrabee to gather his senior staff so they could make critical decisions about next steps.

After a 34-year career in the Coast Guard, from which he had retired as Boston's district commander, Larrabee now had a civilian job that carried enormous responsibility. Every commercial transaction in the Port of New York and New Jersey, the largest container port on the East Coast, was under his domain. He knew Port Authority activities would surely suffer disruptions as a result of what was unfolding at the World Trade Center, and the financial stakes were high. Larrabee's job was to anticipate and mitigate problems as best he could. But before his team could even begin to formulate a plan, the world had changed entirely.

Seventy-two minutes earlier, from his office on the sixty-second floor of the North Tower, Larrabee had felt the building shake so hard that the desks shimmied and framed photos fell off the walls. None of the hundred or so Port Authority staffers had hesitated before gathering their things to leave. "The reaction on everyone's part was, 'Let's get the hell out of here.'"

Though Larrabee had only been working in the building for a year and a half, most of his employees had been present in 1993 when power outages and thick smoke conditions from the explosion in the parking garage had left people in the North Tower blindly groping and choking their way down as many as 106 flights of stairs in the dark. Larrabee understood that his staffers "were already sensitized to the fact that things could go wrong in that building, and that they were up at a really high level." Even on a clear day like this one, the 22-inch-wide windows separated by spandrels and columns that architect Minoru Yamasaki had designed to palliate his fear of heights offered good visibility out, but not down. From the sixty-second floor, it was impossible to see the ground, Larrabee explained. "You just physically couldn't see it. You couldn't tell if it was raining or what it was doing outside."

But on this sunny Tuesday morning, the flaming debris that he watched plunge past the windows on the southwest corner of the building pressed the point that it was time to go. Without knowing that a plane had hit the building, Larrabee picked up his briefcase, wallet, and cell phone, "which I didn't really carry very much in those days," and headed for the stairs. The stairway was well lit and only slightly smoky, and as the Port Authority group descended, workers from different floors converged.

People offered help to those who needed it, and there was no panic. As the evacuees stepped down, firefighters trudged up.

In the years since the bombing, the Port Authority had spent more than $90 million on upgrading physical, structural, and technological enhancements to the twin towers as well as improving fire safety plans and reorganizing the fire-safety and security staffs. Building upgrades had included installing a duplicate power source for fire alarms, emergency lighting, and intercoms, while safety plan improvements included conducting evacuation drills every six months. Due in part to these preparedness efforts, 99 percent of the towers' occupants on the floors below the airplane crashes would manage to escape. In the aftermath of the September 11 attacks, a number of people would report that changes to the buildings' infrastructure and systems had, in fact, facilitated their ability to evacuate.

It took 38 minutes for Larrabee to reach the ground level. Conversation in the stairwells informed him that a plane collision was what had caused the tower to shake. "One of the things that you'd heard if you worked in that building was that even if an airplane hit the building it wouldn't fall down," he explained. "That was the thought in my mind: *As long as I get down to the bottom I'm going to be fine.*" Like so many others that day, Larrabee believed the mythology that had been established during the earliest days of the World Trade Center's development.

⌦⌫⌦

Establishing the towers' ability to survive a plane crash had been just one of many challenges facing the Port Authority during the trade center's decade-long planning and construction process. The idea for the enormous development project had been inspired by a 1939 New York Worlds Fair exhibit called the World Trade Center, which was dedicated to the concept of world peace through trade. As David Rockefeller, grandson of Standard Oil founder John D. Rockefeller, envisioned it, the complex would become the centerpiece of a revitalized Lower Manhattan. To execute his vision, Rockefeller, in 1960, contacted the Port of New York Authority, an agency chartered in 1921 by

New York and New Jersey to build and operate all transportation terminals and facilities within a 25-mile radius of the Statue of Liberty. The Port Authority soon took on the project.

Early on in its development, the complex was conceived not just as the heart of the financial district, but as a major intermodal transportation hub for Lower Manhattan. Plans would include integration and enhancement of the existing railway tunnels (essentially cast-iron tubes) running along the soft riverbed of the Hudson. Since 1909, the Hudson and Manhattan (H&M) Railroad (later known as the H&M Hudson Tubes) had been delivering passengers between Lower Manhattan and Jersey City, transporting a staggering 113,141,729 passengers in its busiest year, 1927.

But ridership soon declined significantly—especially following the openings of the Holland Tunnel, George Washington Bridge, and Lincoln Tunnel, all three of which provided other commuting options. In 1927, the Holland Tunnel, connecting Canal Street in Manhattan with Jersey City's Twelfth and Fourteenth Streets, became the first Hudson River crossing for vehicles. The George Washington Bridge and Lincoln Tunnel soon followed in 1931 and 1937, respectively, increasing traffic flow of automobiles and drawing people away from the railroad.

The World Trade Center project encouraged the Port Authority to take over and renovate the struggling H&M Hudson Tubes in return for the rights to build the new massive complex on the land then occupied by the railway's Lower Manhattan terminal. And thus, in 1962, the Port Authority Trans-Hudson Corporation, or PATH, train was born. The Port Authority unveiled, in January 1964, an architectural plan for the trade center site featuring the world's tallest buildings. Two years later, construction began. The first tenants moved into the North and South Towers in 1970 and 1971, respectively, and the iconic buildings, soon filled with household names, came to represent the powerful and elite.

The twin towers became symbols of American achievement, global trade, the ideals of capitalism, and the quest to be the biggest and the best. Thirty-five years later, though the superskyscrapers seemed to have accepted the brutal assault of airliner intrusion, their deconstruction was already well under way.

Only once Larrabee had reached the North Tower's lobby, where firefighters and evacuees sloshed through several inches of water left by the sprinklers, did he hear that the twin towers had suffered a two-plane attack. Not long after he called his team over to the Marriott's lobby for an emergency meeting, Larrabee heard a large explosion, and he was thrown to the floor. "Everything crumbled around us." He found himself lying in the dark, pinned under a heavy weight. When he felt movement he realized the weight was not only rubble but also a person. A man, a firefighter, had landed on top of him. Although they couldn't see each other through the thick, choking soot, they managed to stay together, working to crawl away from where they'd landed. "I wasn't aware of anyone else around me." Eventually the two men worked their way to a place that seemed flat. Then called by a sense of duty that steered them in opposite directions, they "kind of shook hands and parted ways."

Just like VIP Captain Jerry Grandinetti, Larrabee was wearing, and tasting, and choking on its remains, but still he was unaware that the tower had fallen. In a state of shock, he shambled off, clutching his leather Coach briefcase—a gift he'd received in honor of his Coast Guard retirement. "One of the handles had broken off and I was dragging this thing along for whatever reason," he recalled, still puzzled by his own behavior. "I don't even remember what was in it." As he shuffled through the ashy streets, he remembered the Coast Guard office located due south, at the tip of Manhattan.

He arrived to find a chain-link fence surrounding the facility and headed for a gate. There, Larrabee recognized an officer who had worked for him in Boston a year and a half earlier. "Ed, it's Rick Larrabee. It's Admiral Larrabee," said the retired district commander.

"I'm sorry I don't recognize you," came the response. "You're going to have to show me some ID." Larrabee complied and the officer apologized. "Oh, Admiral. Geez. Come on in." The chagrined officer hadn't been able to make out his admiral's features through the dust.

Sound began trickling through the silence. First the screeching of car alarms. Then voices calling, movement, other people on the ground stumbling. Beginning law student Gina LaPlaca felt someone grabbing at her bare ankles. "You couldn't open your eyes, but it was pitch black anyway. It just felt very heavy." She managed to right herself, to plant her sandaled feet on the street, stretch her palms out in front of her, and stagger through the blackness.

If, in the seconds before 9:58:59 A.M., LaPlaca had been looking at the South Tower instead of at her phone that replied to her every dial attempt with "All circuits are busy," she might have seen the sudden swell of gray smoke bursting from the lowest point of the burning chasm on the east face of the seventy-ninth floor. She might have seen the building's trusses give way, cocking the top 23 floors of the building to the southeast before the lower floors buckled, unleashing cascades of choking debris.

Each face of the towers, framed in structural steel, had been built to withstand hurricane-force winds of 140 miles per hour. Even on an ordinary day the wind load was 30 times greater than the force of a Boeing 767 airliner's impact. It's no wonder the South Tower had stood for so long before the steel spandrel members supporting the cross-braced floors, each with four inches of concrete decking, finally gave way.

And when they did, a rush of energy had hurtled toward LaPlaca, engulfing her. "I felt this gust, this force push me. I lost my feet and flew forward and landed on my face." Head on the pavement, she discovered she couldn't breathe—that the air had mass, substance. "It was like breathing dirt." The blackness total. "At first I felt like there was no one around me—that all of a sudden they had all disappeared—or that I had disappeared."

A few minutes later, though, LaPlaca began to make out the shapes of cars, buildings, the scaffolding over the sidewalk. "I had no idea what I was in or what had happened. I just walked." Then, without warning, someone grabbed her arm. "Don't go that way!" he hollered. His grip prevented her from tumbling down the steps to the Wall Street subway station.

"Thank you," she said. "Thank you so much. Where are we? What is going on?"

He didn't have answers but explained that he and a friend were headed for the South Street Seaport. He urged her to come along. "Keep moving," he said. "I know where we are."

Save for the dust on their clothes the men, both in their thirties, looked like they were "going to work at a bank somewhere," recalled LaPlaca. The trio joined the masses flooding toward Manhattan's eastern shore. Some had cuts and bruises. Some walked through the debris-strewn city streets without shoes. Mouths full of grit, the two men longed for water. A nearby vendor in a silver bagel and donut cart had given away his whole stock of beverages, but LaPlaca pulled a water bottle from her bag. After they drank she used it to flush out her eyes, which had started to swell shut.

Before long they arrived at a commercial fish supplier, M. Slavin & Sons, where workers offered up water hoses, paper towels, and landlines to the gathering crowds. After rinsing herself off, LaPlaca stepped into the office to use the phone. When she couldn't reach her mother at work, she called her grandmother on Long Island and asked her to tell family that she was okay. Then she dialed her parents' home answering machine: "I don't even know if or when you'll hear this because I know you're both at work. But I'm okay. I called Grandma. I told her. I'm trying to figure out what I'm doing." Back outside a woman noticed LaPlaca's torn, wet, and filthy shirt. "She sort of took pity on me," and offered up a coral V-neck pullover that she had in her bag.

LaPlaca longed to go home—even if "home" meant the Gateway Plaza apartment she'd just barely moved into. But with that out of the question, she stuck with the men as they headed for an East Side apartment about two miles away. "The plan, if there was a plan, was to get ourselves up there, walk as far as we could, try to get on transit if it was going up there and regroup." They'd try the phone, watch the news, and attempt to find out what was going on.

About 20 minutes into their trek, one of the guys noticed that a gash along LaPlaca's shin, as well as a cut by her elbow, were bleeding quite a bit. LaPlaca had registered the pain but been too stunned and distracted to grasp that these injuries might require medical attention. At his urging, the three stopped at a community center where someone helped clean and bandage the abrasions. Back outside, the settling dust and distance from the disaster site had allowed daylight to return. "The sun was really irritating my eyes. I was squinting," LaPlaca recalled. "And finally, I couldn't keep my eyes open at all."

"Guys, I'm sorry," she said. "I literally can't keep my eyes open, even one at a time." They took her to the emergency room at nearby Beth Israel Hospital where doctors determined that the corneal abrasions she'd suffered required bandaging her eyes shut. This left LaPlaca blinded in a hospital with strangers in a new city and wondering, *Now what?*

---

New York Waterway Port Captain Michael McPhillips had been standing in the wheelhouse of a ferryboat halfway across the river, when he noticed the South Tower begin to buckle. He'd already made eight round-trip runs ferrying passengers to New Jersey since the first plane hit, while also manning the radio and fielding questions that came at him from all corners.

At 9:45 A.M., when another captain offered to take the helm of *Frank Sinatra* so that McPhillips could focus on operations, the overwhelmed port captain had gladly given up the wheel. He soon wound up conducting operations in the wheelhouse of a different ferry, *George Washington*. Now, seeing the cloud exploding up and out from the shrinking South Tower, he barked out a warning to a captain who had been lining up for his approach to the World Financial Center terminal: "Get the fuck out of there!"

In an instant, the scale of the disaster had magnified, transforming the evacuation-in-progress into a full-blown rescue effort. The cloud rolling past the seawall blanketed the river's surface and blinded boat captains, forcing them to navigate by radar alone. But sometimes even the radar couldn't penetrate the particle-filled air. "We were covered in dust," said McPhillips. "The radar couldn't see through the dust. . . . We were pulling into the dock blind. We were leaving the dock blind. I don't know how it happened, but it happened."

New York Waterway Captain Rick Thornton had departed the Battery just minutes before ten o'clock and was steering north toward Hoboken. As they crossed the river, the crowd aboard ferryboat *Henry Hudson*—which was at, if not over, capacity—went quiet. Then a passenger announced he'd just heard the Pentagon had been hit. Panic spiraled through the crowd as people shouted into cell phones. With both pilothouse doors open, Thornton could hear his passengers' gasps and mutterings, their efforts to grasp the unfolding disaster. Some minutes later, as the boat plied past North Cove, cruising due west of the World Trade Center, Thornton heard a man's voice rise above the din of frantic chatter: "They're gonna collapse!"

Thornton rolled his eyes. *This guy's gonna cause a panic*, he said to himself. *They're never gonna collapse. They're just going to burn out the last upper floors and they'll rebuild them.* Ten seconds later the South Tower began to fold, casting a hush over the crowd. "Everybody on the boat stopped talking, put their cell phones down, and just stared in awe. It was complete silence on the boat. You don't get people off their cell phones," explained Thornton. "Especially New Yorkers. Nobody screamed. Nobody made any kind of a noise. And it was the eeriest reaction you can imagine." The smoke that erupted "was a nightmare." It barreled north and Thornton watched people in the streets sprinting to try to outrun the cloud.

Passengers pushed to the starboard side to see what was happening, and the ferryboat took on a substantial list. The building "came down so majestically it was almost beautiful," said Thornton. "It was beautiful but also terrible to behold." His first thought was of the firefighters. Though he said he's not religious, he instinctively made a sign of the cross, apprehending that "tens, hundreds, thousands, I didn't know how many people, but their lives had just winked out at that very instant." And then he put both hands back on the wheel.

"As all the people were streaming off the boat, every one of them thanked us profusely, thank you, thank you, thank you. As they walked by, they said, 'What are you guys going to do now?'

'We're going back in there.' At that time the first tower collapsed, it looked pretty much like hell on earth. And the people were like, 'I can't believe you guys are going back in there.' But, you know, that's what we had to do."

———— ❧ ————

From the very first moments after the first plane hit, ferry crews had operated as ad hoc first responders. They didn't stop after the South Tower fell. Injured people found their way to the waterfront and ferryboats continued to serve as floating ambulances. Approximately 200 injured would end up transported aboard New York Waterway ferries by day's end. McPhillips recalled a man who boarded the ferry in a white shirt and dark pants that were "literally melted" to his body. "He was covered with the dust. His clothes were melted to him and it started to boil the skin. It started to swell." The man—perhaps Kenneth Summers, perhaps another of the fireball's victims—had suffered burns over his whole body, and his skin reminded McPhillips of a wax museum statue that had gotten too hot. The ferry delivered him across the river to a makeshift triage center being laid out by rescue workers along the Jersey waterfront.

Despite the unprecedented scale of this disaster, mariners' "jack of all trades" capabilities proved essential in the aftermath of the attacks. McPhillips had begun the morning as a port captain tracking boat schedules. But soon he was pulling glass shards from a man's forearm and then wrapping it with gauze from the boat's first aid kit to staunch the bleeding. In some sense, mariners were no different from other civilians who simply brought their ordinary skills to an extraordinary situation, breaking an unmanageable set of circumstances into manageable pieces and tackling them one by one.

Given that 85 percent of our nation's critical infrastructure is controlled not by government but by the private sector, the "first" first responders in most catastrophes, say disaster researchers, are most often civilians. Yet even as civilians, the boatmen and boatwomen of New York harbor were particularly well equipped to serve the public in key ways.

For better or worse, boats and ships—especially oceangoing vessels—often operate in relative isolation, existing as self-contained entities. If a fire breaks out while a vessel is under way, having crew members skilled in shipboard fire suppression is critical to the survival of the vessel and all those aboard. Similarly, rapid response to a medical emergency becomes a matter of life or death.

Ever since the Steamboat Act of 1852, federal law has required the licensure of pilots and engineers working aboard certain vessels carrying passengers for hire. Since 1942, the Coast Guard has been responsible for overseeing all functions of maritime safety, including vessel inspections and mariner certification.

Although the specific prerequisites have changed over time, attaining a Coast Guard "ticket" requires merchant mariners to complete training and earn certifications in first aid, CPR, and shipboard firefighting, among other specialized areas. Additionally, Coast Guard license testing includes whole sections on vessel safety requirements established in the Code of Federal Regulations (CFRs), a 200-volume set of rulebooks totaling thousands of pages that governs every aspect of maritime work. Among the provisions are specific protocols for abandon ship and man-overboard drills. According to CFR 122.520, "The master [the properly licensed individual having command of the vessel] shall conduct sufficient drills and give sufficient instructions to make sure that all crew members are familiar with their duties during emergencies that necessitate abandoning ship or the recovery of persons who have fallen overboard."

So, every month, year after year, during Coast Guard-required man-overboard drills, New York Waterway deckhands had practiced retrieving an aluminum ladder, hooking it through notches in the bow as they hung it over the side, and climbing down the seven feet from the deck to the waterline to help imaginary swimmers begin their ascent. On this morning, however, the people who'd gone overboard were real, and all that training was put to the test. McPhillips and the crew aboard the ferryboat *George Washington* pulled at least six people from the water between North and South Coves—the same stretch of the Hudson where

Wiggs and Lacey had been fighting strong currents. Other Waterway boats did the same.

Because of the safety protocols followed aboard New York
Waterway ferryboats, execution of water rescues was "very simple," McPhillips explained. "It wasn't a big deal." At least not pro-
cedurally. The ferry crews were ready, willing, and able to quickly
pluck out people who ended up waving their arms for help shortly
after they hit the river that McPhillips described as "brutal."

After one water rescue, McPhillips recalled, the deck crew
didn't bother to stow the ladder. Instead the boat proceeded
straight to the seawall north of the terminal where they saw dock
builder Paul Amico and others helping people over the railing,
down ladders, and onto the boats.

---

Paul Amico had been in the wheelhouse of a Waterway ferry
approaching the World Financial Center terminal when the South
Tower gave way. If he'd heard McPhillips's warning as the tower
came down, the ferry's captain didn't heed it. Despite the white-
out conditions, the boat kept coming. Amico watched the captain
maneuver in by radar.

On their way across the Hudson, the two had been discussing
the morning's conditions. "The only thing I was thinking about
was, *We're going to need to get people out,*" recalled Amico. "I
was asking the captain about volumes, who was out there on the
river—what boats were out there, what captains were out there."
As the main fabricator of New York Waterway's dockside infrastructure, Amico knew most of them by name.

When they reached Manhattan, Amico stepped onto the blue
barge that served as Waterway's loading platform, its glass walls
and white circus-tent roof plastered with powder. The power had
gone out and passengers were panicking. "We need to get off!"
"You need to get me off now!" "Don't wait for anyone else," they
urged, choking, their faces caked with dust.

Their urgency might have given Amico cause to reconsider
disembarking on Manhattan Island while everyone else clam-
ored to get off. But he remained clear in his objective. "Civilians

are comfortable on the land. Captains are comfortable on the water. I'm comfortable with one foot on the boat and one foot on the land. That's where I work. So that's where I needed to be." Amico decided that the best help he could provide was to serve as a bridge. "*You've got the fire and police over there. Where I can probably help the best is right here on the water's edge,*" he recalled thinking. "Let the plumbers do the plumbing."

He asked the captain to spread the word that he had a hand-held marine radio. He knew that land-based fire companies and police had no means of communicating with the ferryboats, and he aimed to span that gap, helping to direct civilians to the river—their quickest means of escape.

Now that the terminal was overwhelmed with soot, Waterway director of operations Johansen had begun directing waiting passengers farther north along the seawall where the air was clearer. From the wheelhouse of the *George Washington*, meanwhile, Michael McPhillips instructed captains to pick up people wherever they could do so safely. As shallow-draft bow-loaders, the New York Waterway ferries could pull up and take on passengers virtually anywhere, which proved hugely advantageous as the day unfolded.

Amico was well aware that only two New York Waterway ferry terminals existed in Lower Manhattan: the World Financial Center terminal, fewer than 1,000 feet from the twin towers; and Pier 11, located around the tip of Manhattan on the East River. He took it upon himself to help figure out more viable options.

"I'm looking at the water's edge and saying, where else can I get Waterway's boats in and out? That's my concern." Just south of the barge, he ran into a police sergeant trying to calm people and keep them moving north. Amico explained that he had communication with the boats via VHF and the officer spread the word. Throngs of injured civilians and firefighters flocked to the waterfront.

With the help of Amico and Johansen on land, deckhands on each ferry facilitated boarding by hooking the boats' steel man-overboard ladders over the seawall railings so they sloped down the six feet or so to the deck at an easy 45-degree angle. Most passengers were able to scale the railings and descend the ladders to board the boats, but those who weren't received further assistance.

"If we had injured, we actually slid them down the ladder," Amico recalled. Even people in wheelchairs were able to board thanks to the cooperation of deckhands and other riders. "We had enough civilians to help. It was one of those things, no one stood back, whether civilian or employee," said Amico. Once a boat had injured aboard, the captain would turn and go. Another boat would glide in behind it. "At one point we were loading three or four boats at a time." And the people kept coming.

CHAPTER **6**

# "We're in the water!"

THAT MANHATTAN IS an island—a fact easily forgotten by modern day New Yorkers and visitors alike—was unmissable in the nineteenth century when, before bridges and tunnels, boats were the only means of travel on or off. The earliest crossings had been made by rowboats and periaugers (sailing craft with the option of oar-power supplementation). That held true until July 2, 1812, when Robert Fulton inaugurated steam-powered ferry service across the Hudson River between Manhattan and New Jersey aboard the double-ended steamboat *Jersey*. The new, oddly configured steamboat's regular 20-minute crossings launched the first-ever mechanically powered ferryboat service.

After that July day, steam-powered ferry services multiplied. By 1860, 11 different companies offered no fewer than 20 ferry routes to and from Manhattan. The early 1900s were perhaps the busiest years for New York harbor ferries, as steel-hull propeller boats became more common and city-run service was established. But as options for reaching the island expanded, ferry use began to dwindle.

In 1936, 117 ferryboats plied the waters of New York harbor—64 percent of them railroad-related or privately operated. But by 1975, just nine boats remained in operation, all of them run by the City of New York. Ridership decreased from 112.6 million in 1936 to about 20 million in 1975. As had happened with the Hudson and Manhattan (H&M) Railroad, the construction of bridges and vehicle tunnels drew commuters away from waterborne transit. In response to sharply reduced need, the last of the cross-Hudson ferries ended service in 1967, leaving the publicly owned Staten Island Ferry as the city's oldest, largest, and last standing ferry service.

For two decades, no cross-Hudson ferry existed. Then, in the mid-80s, the ridership battles between ferries and bridges and tunnels came full circle. With riverside developments cropping up along the Jersey waterfront, trucking company owner Arthur Imperatore recognized a new business opportunity. Bridges and tunnels were operating at peak capacity during commuter hours, which meant a waterborne transportation alternative—especially one offering a compelling four-minute crossing—could gain wide appeal. And so, in 1986, the *Port Imperial* ferry service was born, operating between Weehawken, New Jersey, and West Thirty-eighth Street, Manhattan.

Soon after, Imperatore's company submitted the winning bid to the Port Authority in response to its request for an operator to restore ferry service to the World Trade Center, via the World Financial Center terminal. Thus, more than 75 years after the idea of a public ferry service was inaugurated in New York City, a renewed trend toward private ferries began.

Later, Imperatore's expanding company was renamed New York Waterway, and by 1991, seven ferry routes carried more than 16,000 passengers daily. In 2000, ridership reached 32,000. The growing market soon attracted newcomers, including SeaStreak, sister company of Hoverspeed, an operator of English Channel ferries. On September 11, 2001, SeaStreak also lent its assets to the evacuation effort.

---

Tens of thousands of people were already streaming away from Manhattan on foot over bridges when, at 11:02 A.M., then-Mayor Rudolph Giuliani called upon everyone south of Canal Street to "get out." "Walk slowly and carefully," he said. "If you can't figure what else to do, just walk north." If this sounds vague, that's because it was. There was no plan. Even the planners had no plan for what was unfolding in Lower Manhattan.

"I'm a planner," explained U.S. Coast Guard Lieutenant Commander Kevin Gately in an internal oral history interview conducted eight months after the attacks. On September 11 he'd been a reservist for nearly 22 years, and his job with Activities New York's Waterways Management Division was planning periodic search and rescue and port readiness assessment exercises. The closest exercise approximation to the September 11 attacks, he conceded, was a series sponsored by the New Jersey Office of Emergency Management that had begun in the spring of 2000. The exercise had played out responses to a supposed terrorist attack on a Port Authority facility using a weapon of mass destruction.

When the events of that morning actually unfolded, he explained, "Our port security response was basically exactly what had been postulated in the exercise." But there was one significant difference: "The evacuation problem. That was completely unanticipated. That entire thing was improvised on the spot." The total evacuation of Lower Manhattan, he reiterated, had never been envisioned, was never dreamt of in our philosophy."

When the South Tower came down, Lieutenant Michael Day was on Staten Island standing in the Coast Guard Command Center, "riveted" to a big-screen television broadcasting CNN. "We got reports there were people congregating on the lower tip of Manhattan," he recalled. "That's when it really kicked in—when the first tower collapsed." VTS cameras showed people stacking up at the shoreline.

Boats of all kinds amassed along the water's edge, cramming their decks and interior spaces with evacuees, trying to deliver as many people off the island as possible. This unregulated effort raised Coast Guard concerns that overcrowding would cause problems on the water.

The acting captain of the port, Deputy Commander Patrick Harris, had very strategically perched himself on a high stool to coordinate the Activities New York response surrounded by representatives from all relevant departments. Haunted by visions from 1980 of a Coast Guard boat that he'd seen "almost turning turtle" after being overloaded with refugees during the Cuban boat lift, Harris dispatched to "highly visible rallying points" a cadre of marine inspectors and investigators "with good strong command voices" who were knowledgeable about vessel capacities to ensure order and safety aboard ferries and to prevent other boat operators from loading unsafe numbers of passengers.

"We weren't as concerned about the fast ferries and those guys because they knew what they could do safely for passengers," he explained. "What we were really concerned with were the tugboats and the little private vessels—the guys that don't normally carry passengers."

Reports from on-scene mariners—the operators of tugs, small boats, ferries, and other vessels who'd made their way to Manhattan's shores almost immediately after the planes hit—continued to pour in, helping to augment what Coast Guard personnel at the VTS could see on-screen. But as the scale of the disaster compounded, the need for on-scene leadership became clear. Day would head out with a small team. But instead of using a Coast Guard vessel, Day decided to accept Sandy Hook Pilot Andrew McGovern's offer for a boat.

The everyday job of the (currently 75 active) highly trained men and women of the Sandy Hook Pilots Association is to board all designated vessels as they enter or leave New York harbor, guiding them safely through the port. For more than 300 years, these local navigation experts have met schooners, steamships, and oceangoing vessels of all sorts at the entrance to the port to guide incoming ships across a series of shoals, called the Bar of Sandy Hook, that separate New York harbor from the Atlantic Ocean.

In 1694, even before New York became a state, the then-colony appointed the first local mariners as Sandy Hook Pilots, employing a term derived from the Dutch words *pijl* (pole) and *lood* (lead), which describe an early tool used to sound depths and chart waters. Initially these pilots operated independently, racing to be the first to reach a vessel and thereby secure the job of applying their local knowledge of tides, currents, shoals, and navigational hazards to guide a ship safely into port. In 1895, however, pilots from New York and New Jersey joined forces and established a regular working rotation. In 2015, the Sandy Hook Pilots made more than 10,000 trips aboard tankers, yachts, cargo, and cruise ships. They facilitated delivery of roughly 95 percent of all cargo entering the port.

All vessels longer than 100 feet that are flying a foreign flag or carrying foreign cargo are now legally required to have a licensed pilot aboard while traversing the harbor. This means that 24 hours a day, 365 days a year, in all weather conditions and port circumstances, Sandy Hook Pilots stand ready to board passenger liners, freighters, tankers, and other large ships on the open sea at the mouth of the harbor by stepping off the deck of a 53-foot aluminum launch onto the rungs of a ladder hung at midship. The work can be extremely dangerous. As the Sandy Hook Pilots Association president, Captain John Oldmixon, put it, "The chances of getting hurt are great, and the chances of you dying are significant if you mess up, or something goes wrong, or the ladder's not rigged right."

Securing the honor of serving in this precarious position is no easy feat. Until recently one had to know someone to land an apprenticeship. Times have changed somewhat, but still very few applicants are accepted into the association's rigorous five-year training program, which concludes with a four-day exam during which apprentices must reproduce from memory sections of nautical charts including every depth and buoy as well as each rock, reef, shoal, pipeline, and cable. Passing this test opens the door to an additional seven years of training as a deputy pilot before earning the designation (and salary) of full branch pilot. On September 11, the pilots not only knew where boats could safely tie up or load passengers, based on depths, currents, and hidden hazards, they also were familiar—from their work in the harbor every day—with the boats, the companies, and the mariners.

Surely their encyclopedic knowledge of the port and its people could be useful at a time like this. The question was, just how exactly? At this moment, no one was exactly sure. "There wasn't a preplanned response: This is what we do for two planes crashing into the towers," explained Day. Instead, "people were scurrying around" trying to figure out next steps.

Pilot McGovern had been driving to Manhattan for a Harbor Ops Committee meeting when the sight of the World Trade Center in flames made him reroute, beelining for the Fort Wadsworth Coast Guard Station where he knew he could get more information and offer up assistance. All our resources are at your disposal, McGovern had told Commander Daniel Ronan when he arrived.

One invaluable resource the pilots could provide was a mobile operating platform for coordinating the Coast Guard's on-scene response. Day agreed with McGovern that the 185-foot pilot boat *New York* would offer an ideal vessel for facilitating the maritime evacuation already under way, readily allowing for pilot and Coast Guard collaboration. Normally functioning as a combination command post and floating hotel, the highly maneuverable *New York* was well suited to staying on station for extended periods and offered a large wheelhouse with 360-degree views that was fully equipped with radar, radios, and other communications equipment.

In addition to the vessel itself, Day recognized the important contribution that the pilots' rich knowledge base, depth of experience, and strength of relationships with other mariners would bring to this emergency effort. He explained his highly unorthodox choice to join forces and use a non-Coast Guard asset as the base for Coast Guard activity in simple terms: the Sandy Hook Pilots "know that port like it's nobody's business."

Before Day set out to drive the short distance to the pilot station a few piers north, he pulled together paperwork, including nautical charts of the harbor and a copy of the plans that the Coast Guard had spent two years developing for the International Naval Review and Operation Sail (OpSail) event from the previous year.

On July 4, 2000, New York City had played host to a parade of tall sailing ships, naval vessels, yachts, and other ships from all around the world in what was believed to be the largest-ever port gathering, which included hundreds of security vessels as well as tens of thousands of pleasure craft. Managing the harbor traffic that day had presented VTS operators with the most demanding test in the center's history. Day thought the OpSail plans, which included medical and logistic staging procedures, might prove valuable as he set out across the harbor toward the unknown.

As it turned out, the OpSail event itself was already helping some mariners meet the challenges of the evacuation through the practical experience it had granted. During OpSail, instead of their usual 68 daily dockings at the company's own slips, New York Waterway captains moved 70,000 soldiers a day, often in unfamiliar territory. "We had to really pull into some bizarre places and offload the soldiers, [like] the sides of ships in a six-knot current," explained Port Captain Michael McPhillips. "I really think the captains gained a lot more experience doing that." Although the particulars of mariners' work on September 11 were unprecedented, OpSail preparations at least offered some guidance.

As he stood in the wheelhouse of the pilot boat *New York*, bound for Manhattan Island, Day had no concept that he and his team would soon be facilitating the largest waterborne evacuation in history. Or that he'd lose contact with his command.

—⚬⚬⚬—

*At least I'll have a fighting chance in the river*, Karen Lacey thought as she hovered at the edge of the seawall, preparing to jump. *I can swim. I can tread water. I'm an athlete. I'm not going to be stuck on the top of a building, hanging out of a window. I'm not going to be underground with a building collapsing on me. I'll have a fighting chance.*

From the time that she and Tammy Wiggs had left their other colleagues on the street corner a few blocks from the New York Stock Exchange, Lacey had made steering clear of buildings a priority. She hugged the shoreline as best she could on her way toward the World Financial Center ferry terminal, determined to get home to Hoboken. Now, as the pulverized tower plowed toward her, rolling like magma through the gaps between buildings and onto the waterfront plaza, the river promised salvation.

The sky went black as Lacey stood outside the rail. Chalky particles burned her throat. *I'm going in*, she decided, and plunged.

When she kicked herself back to the surface, she drew a choking breath and then buried her face back in the river, bobbing up and down half a dozen times before the sky changed from black to gray.

The drop to the river had been farther than she expected, and the current much stronger. She quickly kicked off her pumps, which were now making their way downstream, but she refused to drop the bag slung over her shoulder. Not only did it contain her wallet, the keys to her apartment, and tickets to that night's Broadway performance of *The Producers*, but the Coach tote was her second—a $400 investment she'd made to replace her first: a graduation present that had been ripped off at a bar. She clung to the seawall and to the bag, kicking to stay afloat.

She heard Tammy Wiggs screaming, but said nothing.

"Now, I'm out to lunch. Now I'm spent. Now, I can't believe that we're here," she recalled. "I was trying to regroup. Maybe when the fog lifted, when the dust went away, I would get my bearings and start all over again but at that point . . ."

"We're in the water! We're in the water!" Wiggs yelled.

A gruff voice called back through the cloud, "Who's in the water?"

Lacey was farther north along the seawall than Wiggs and a good distance from the fireboat, so it took a while before she could see the boat, the ladder, or the bear of a man whose voice, low and booming, with a thick New York accent, served as a beacon in the murk.

The man calling down from the bow of fireboat *John D. McKean* might well have been firefighter Billy Gillman. It was Gillman's voice, at least, that rang out across the deck announcing to the rest of the *McKean* crew that two women were in the water. Engineer Gulmar Parga heard his call, as did wiper Greg Woods. Immediately Woods, an experienced lifeguard, grasped the danger of the situation. If either woman lost her grip on the concrete, the current would pull her downstream toward where the boat's hull banged against the seawall. She would be crushed.

Woods set off to collect the boat's Jacob's ladder, the best tool to bridge the gap between the river's surface and the deck. Meanwhile, someone on deck threw a rope over the side. Wiggs heard talk of a ladder but thought that the people on deck were saying they couldn't find one. With her fingertips still digging into a joint in the concrete seawall, Wiggs considered the line, thick as a Coke can with a loop at the end, as her only chance at rescue. But getting it into her hands wasn't going to be easy. The rope bobbed about three feet away. To reach it, she'd have to let go of the wall.

"All I could picture was getting sucked in between the boat and the seawall," she recalled. "It was all about timing . . . One, two, three, let go, push off, and you have one chance of grabbing this line because the current was ripping."

Wiggs let go. She pushed off. She caught the rope. Worried she didn't have much strength left, she decided to slip her legs through the loop to sit in it like a seat, and catch her breath. But as she kicked at it with her bare foot, the loop pulled through. Wiggs lost her grip on the line for a second but managed to snatch it back. She hollered up to the boat. "Give me more slack!"

But the people on the bow couldn't hear her clearly. Instead of feeding her more loose line they called out encouragements: "No ma'am, don't let go! Don't give up! Hold on."

Wiggs yelled up again, louder this time. "No. Give me some SLACK and I'll tie a knot that will hold!" Years later she'd laugh at herself recalling the moment. ("Here I am talking smack to the guy that's trying to save me.")

Finally, someone slacked out the line and Wiggs applied her sailor's knowledge to make a loop. Even as she treaded water, working with rope that was five times the size of any she'd ever before handled, Wiggs was able to tie a bowline knot that held. She put both legs through, sat in the loop, and the people on deck began yanking her out of the water.

Wiggs was most of the way up the side of the boat when, at last, the Jacob's ladder appeared over the side. She used it to step up the last few rungs to the cap rail. Now it was Karen Lacey's turn.

After she saw Wiggs swing her legs over the cap rail of the fireboat, Lacey inched her fingers down the concrete slab to get closer to the ladder, then pushed off to grab it. But even with her hands wrapped around the ladder's rope rails, she was still far from safe.

"The current was super strong and the ladder was super wiggly," Lacey recalled. "I can't get up the damned thing."

Although low water had hit the Battery at 8:50 A.M., the currents in this portion of the Hudson were determined by more than just the tide. Sometimes the current continued to pull downstream even as the flood tide began. Such were the conditions on the morning of September 11; many mariners reported a "ripping" ebb well into the ten o'clock hour.

As it dangled from the cap rail, the rope ladder with orange plastic rungs draped against the curve of the hull where it narrowed near the waterline. Simultaneously, the ebb pulled the lowest rungs downstream. The curled and bobbing ladder offered Lacey no leverage to gain her footing. Relying on just upper-body strength to haul herself out of the water proved impossible, and clinging to the ladder brought her even closer to the point where the hull slammed against the seawall. Lacey swayed a few feet from the point of impact.

"Come on. You can do it," the men called down to her.

"I can't," she yelled back. "So they're screaming at me: 'Drop the bag. Drop the bag.' And I was like, 'I'm not gonna.' 'Lady,' they said, 'drop the bag.'" *I can't believe I'm losing another one of these things*, she thought as she pulled the tote off her shoulder and let it go.

But bag or no bag, athlete or not, Lacey was tired. She couldn't lift herself up. Woods, the part-time lifeguard, jumped in after her.

"I saw his head bobbing in the water, and I was like, *Good idea!*" recalled marine engineer Gulmar Parga. He followed close behind, climbing down the pad eyes supporting the bow fender until he reached the water. He grabbed the ladder's rope side, pulling it taut.

Telecommunications specialist Rich Varela, the civilian who had boarded the boat only a few minutes earlier and was now bare-chested with a piece of shirt tied around his face, had been standing on the bow beside the lifeguard. Now he hung over the side to help to stabilize the ladder from above.

Woods dove underwater. In a single swooping movement that left those watching from the deck somewhat awestruck, Woods hoisted Lacey on his shoulders and placed her feet on a ladder rung that Parga was bracing from the waterline and Varela was steadying from above. Once Lacey's feet were planted, she was able to climb enough rungs that Varela and others on deck could reach her arms and help her the rest of the way.

Finally out of the water, Lacey yanked her skirt back down over her shredded stockings, less embarrassed by the exposure than her inability to climb the ladder. Before her stood the man—wearing bunker pants, his glasses covered with a gray film—whose voice had called out through the cloud. Lacey gave him the first of the umpteen thank-yous she would deliver before deboarding in Jersey City. "I probably thanked him—conservatively—two thousand times. That's all I said the whole way up the ladder, down across the river, when I got off the boat was thank you."

CHAPTER *7*

# "Gray ghosts"

AT 10:28 A.M., the churning black smoke cloaking the top of the North Tower swelled, suddenly thicker and blacker. The upper floors of the superskyscraper cocked back, cracking open the west face of the building. For an instant the fires feasted, gorging themselves on the fresh supply of oxygen—orange tongues of flame licking out at the sky. And then, seemingly in slow motion, everything above crushed everything below.

Sean Kennedy watched it happen from the open-air helm of his thrill-ride speedboat, the *Chelsea Screamer*. "It started slow, breaking itself apart from the top," he later explained in his languid Mississippi lilt. At one point, when the radio antenna that had stolen his focus seemed to pause in midair, he thought: *Don't fall! Don't fall! . . . Stop! Stop!* But the building didn't stop. It continued to cave. "It's coming down and there's a point where you can't say anything more. It's happened." Kennedy watched the spire plunge until it was engulfed in smoke and dust. He watched sections of the tower's iconic pinstripe columns slice through the southeast corner of 3 World Financial Center as metal fragments shot through the glass dome of the Winter Garden.

Kennedy, a longtime captain and charter-yacht owner who'd spent a lifetime on the water, was holding station just offshore of the Winter Garden, about 1,500 feet away from 1 World Trade Center. That particular distance was no accident. Kennedy had still been on land at 9:58 A.M., running down the West Side Highway on his way to the *Screamer*'s berth at Chelsea Piers, when 2 World Trade Center collapsed out of view. He didn't know how the tower had fallen, whether it had toppled "like a pine tree" or folded in on itself. Once he was out on the water he kept a careful distance.

On most days the *Chelsea Screamer* offered "splash and dash scenic adventures" around New York harbor. But today the 56-passenger tour boat was being used as a floating camera platform for a news agency crew looking to capture footage of the disaster. Three seconds before the building came down, Kennedy had been gaping in horror at the sight of bodies falling from the blazing North Tower. "A person!" he cried, his usual drawl overtaken by a tight, pinched screech. "Another person!"

"Holy sh—God! Mother of God!" shouted Kennedy's friend, crewmate, and fellow charter captain Greg Freitas, as the debris cloud mushroomed up, coursing riverine through every available opening, choking nearby buildings, branching out into tributaries, clogging every crevice, blanketing whole neighborhoods with the same stinging powder that the South Tower had unleashed a half hour earlier.

The building had twisted, unleashing a gale of wind—a burst of 55 million cubic feet of air—sending steel trusses screeching, glass erupting, columns crashing. Somehow, the noise made by all this destruction transported Kennedy back to his hometown in Biloxi, to the tracks where passing trains often stopped him on his way to school. While waiting to cross he'd listen to the clack of wheels. The sound that this mammoth building made as it crumbled— "kind of a continuous eruption of breakage"—reminded him of the thumps, clangs, and rattles of a string of rickety boxcars careening by at close range.

Minutes after the pulverized remnants of 1 World Trade Center settled out of the air along Manhattan's western shore, Kennedy caught sight of a Port Authority police officer waving him over to the shoreline. "Start evacuating people!" he ordered. "Anybody that can get over here we're gonna evacuate them." Kennedy complied. Though the bow of his speedboat sat well below the level of the loading platform, he nosed the vessel into a slip on the north side of New York Waterway's World Financial Center terminal to pick up anyone needing transport.

Spurred on by *Screamer* crew member Greg Freitas's indelicate urging, a handful of businessmen in white shirts and neckties bolted across the barge toward the speedboat. "Come on guys. Anybody coming? Get your ass over here, now. Now!" barked Freitas. "Come on. Come on! I want you to hold my hand and come on board. Get inside. Anybody else? Come on. Let's GO! Hold my hand. Get in. One at a time . . ."

Next Kennedy steered the boat south. Like the people trapped in the upper floors of the twin towers who had clustered at the windows, desperate for air, those caught in the avalanche of debris in Lower Manhattan fled to the water's edge, frantically trying to escape the choking cloud.

As he pulled into South Cove, a small rectangular notch cut out of Manhattan's western shore about 1,500 feet from the World Trade Center complex, Kennedy laid eyes on the people who'd been caught in that avalanche. "It looked like you had taken the ash from a fire and put it in a bucket and dumped it over them," Kennedy recalled. The dust clung to their clothes, to their bags and briefcases. People who had dressed in white that morning were now cloaked in a dark gray. When the *Chelsea Screamer* arrived, several police boats were already boarding passengers.

Kennedy pulled the *Screamer* into the cove, tying up alongside an NYPD launch, and passengers immediately began streaming aboard. Some evacuees stepping onto the bow of the police boat kept going to that vessel's recessed stern deck: a disoriented firefighter needed help donning a life preserver. A tall man in cargo shorts with dust-coated glasses and a towel around his neck pulled a dog on a leash. A shorter man wore black-and-white striped chef's pants.

Others, meanwhile, crossed from the bow of the launch onto the stern of the *Screamer*. Kennedy grabbed people's hands as they boarded, offering stability as they stepped across the ever-changing gap created by the two boats bobbing against each other. A young woman with long wavy blond hair toting a cat in a black purse cupped a cloth over her mouth. A round, middle-aged man in shorts with white hair and dark eyebrows carried a backpack. A preschooler in a yellow T-shirt clung tightly to a big woman in a baseball cap, his arms never loosening their grip around her neck.

At one point a man called down to the *Screamer* from Launch 3. "Does anybody have the baby?"

"Nobody has it," another man called back from the bow. A mother and her baby had been separated during boarding, Kennedy explained. "The baby went into the policeman's hand onto the police boat and she went into our boat," he said, adding that the two were quickly reunited.

More women continued to board with small children. A slender woman in a blue T-shirt passed a toddler to Kennedy before straddling the gap. A large woman in a pale yellow shirt handed over a chubby baby wearing short pants and squinting in the sun. Neither seemed to have been caught in the dust. Once the woman got her footing, she collected the infant and pulled him in tight.

---

Many people caught up in the unfolding catastrophe also had the duty of protecting children. Parents, teachers, daycare workers, and sitters were all forced to navigate their way through the danger while simultaneously soothing their frightened charges. Florence Fox, a 32-year-old nanny from Zambia, was one such person.

Nearly two hours earlier, at 8:45 A.M., in a Battery Park City townhouse on Albany Street a few blocks southwest of the South Tower, four-year-old Kitten was pestering her. "Let's go, Florence. Let's *go-o*," the girl mewled. Every Tuesday morning the two attended a story hour at the Borders bookstore in 5 World Trade Center, on the northeastern corner of the complex at the corner of Church and Vesey Streets. "Jeez, Kitten. Let me finish my bagel," Fox responded. "We're gonna go. We're gonna go."

Nannying came naturally to Fox, who'd helped raise her eight younger siblings. She had been caring for the girl she called "Kitten" since Kate Silverton was six weeks old. "I didn't look at Kitten like it was my job," she explained. "I treated her like my own child. I think she felt the same. She was very attached to me. She would tell me that she loved me."

Fox had just popped the last bite of bagel in her mouth when she heard an unfathomable sound. "I heard this noise. A big boom. Everything shook." She unlatched the front door of the house that opened directly onto the street. "I saw smoke. People were just screaming." Fox went inside and clicked on the television to find out what was going on, but quickly switched it back off. "I had to think of Kate. I didn't want her to see. I didn't want her to be freaked out." The phone rang. The girl's mother, Susan Silverton, had learned about the plane just moments after it hit and called to instruct Fox to stay inside until she returned home.

To explain to the child why they couldn't go to the bookstore, Fox made up a story. She distracted her with crayons and coloring books, arranging everything on a table before heading upstairs to watch the bedroom television out of view. Outside, the sounds of sirens and chaos grew louder, drawing Fox back downstairs to peek out the front door.

"All these people were dripping with blood, wailing and screaming. They were talking about people jumping." Someone yelled, *Another one! Another one!* and Fox heard a high-pitched peal streak through the sky. She slammed the door and ran back upstairs to the television. On-screen, a jet pierced through the south face of 2 World Trade Center just as the townhouse began to tremble in the wake of a percussive boom. Fox fell to her knees, shaking. *What do I do? I have this child.*

Back downstairs she tried to dial the girl's mother, but couldn't get through. Feeling the weight of a mother's trust, Fox was torn about whether to stay or go. Outside, the mayhem roared louder. "Florence, what's that noise?" There was no hiding the look on Fox's face. "She could see I was scared." For nearly an hour Fox struggled with her decision.

Then suddenly another massive concussion shook the house. *Oh my God*, thought Fox. *Now they've started bombing.* She opened the front door to see a wall of white debris moving at her "like a tsunami."

"Kitten, come over here now!" Fox screamed and the girl came running. She scooped her up in her arms and ran down the front steps. Neither had on shoes. "I don't even remember closing the door to the house," said Fox. Instantly they were plastered with debris. The child started to shiver and weep. "Don't cry," Fox told her. "It will be fine. Put your head in my breast and don't look."

Kitten buried her face against her nanny's chest, the woman's skin bare above her red scoop-neck T-shirt. Her small arms gripped Fox's shoulders, her little legs clenching at her waist as the woman fled barefoot through the street, trying to outrun the cloud. Like most people, Fox had no concept that the towers could fall. She assumed the city was being bombed. She didn't want to stop running but before long the powder burned her face and clouded up her eyes until she couldn't see. Time and again she paused for a second to wipe her eyes before continuing south on South End Avenue.

When at last she'd run far enough that the dust began to settle she could see that the neighborhood in which she'd worked for four years had been blanketed in a gray-white snow. She saw a man lying on the ground, wailing. She kicked him. "Get up!" she demanded. "Look at me," she said. "I have a child and I'm running. You have to get up. Let's go." She meant it as encouragement. And the prodding worked. The man got up and also began to run.

Up ahead Fox spotted people taking cover in a restaurant and she followed them inside. As she stood, still holding onto Kitten, people around her chattered, grasping at threads of information they hoped might explain what was unfolding outside the door. All conversation stopped short when a second rumble shook the earth. Fox closed her eyes. Screams erupted all around. "We thought they were bombs," Fox explained. "At this point people just lost it, just like wailing and crying." Kate bawled too. "Florence! Florence!" she called.

"I said, 'Kitten, it's okay. We'll be fine. It's okay.'" In that moment, staying strong for the little girl in her care was what propped Fox up to keep going. "She trusted me," the nanny explained. "Even with how she held onto me, she knew that I was going to take care of her."

With all the hysteria, Fox couldn't stay in the restaurant. "Up to this point, Kitten was scared but she wasn't subjected to other people screaming, and seeing fear." Fox knew she had to protect her from the crowd. "I cannot let her see this." Fox did not yet know how traumatizing this experience would wind up being for the little girl in her charge, but she was determined to do whatever she could to protect her.

Fox waited for the second wave of soot to settle before hitting the street once again. "I wiped my eyes. I went outside. And when I went outside I saw this little police boat."

---

"Gray ghosts." That was what the hoards of fraught, powder-plastered people looked like to Tony Sirvent as he nosed the police launch into South Cove for the first time. Known as a "cool customer," Sirvent was the NYPD Harbor Unit's senior pilot. For 30 years he had been bringing to his work both a commitment to serve and a no-nonsense, get-it-done approach. Today would be no different. That morning Sirvent's duty assignment was as pilot of the NYPD's 52-foot aluminum launch—known as Launch 9 or *Harbor Charlie*—stationed at the Harbor Unit's headquarters at the Brooklyn Army Terminal in Sunset Park, Brooklyn. That was where he had been when the planes hit.

Once known as the U.S. Army Military Ocean Terminal, the massive, 4-million-square-foot complex was built in only 17 months. From its completion in September of 1919 through World War II, the facility served as the nation's largest military supply base. Employing more than 20,000 military and civilian personnel, the site was the headquarters for the New York Port of Embarkation, a regional operation that moved 3.2 million troops and 37 million tons of military supplies to fronts across the globe.

Now, 56 years after World War II had ended, the facility where so many troops had shipped off would begin receiving evacuees fleeing a war zone right here at home, just five miles north in New York harbor. But Sirvent didn't yet know that when he and his three-person crew left the Harbor Unit base and went gunning toward Lower Manhattan. The launch had almost reached the southern tip of Governor's Island when the South Tower caved. Wind pulling the debris cloud to the southeast gave the officers a clear view of the devastation as they approached South Cove, where clusters of people had begun amassing along the water's edge.

As Sirvent steered into the notch, dust-covered people swarmed toward the boat, surging forward, pressing themselves against the railings, some scaling the wooden fences that separated the land from the water. "All right. Billy, get a line on those fences," Sirvent called to his newest crew member, Officer William Chartier, who'd joined the Harbor Unit only three months earlier.

At first Chartier didn't understand what the pilot had in mind. He tied a rope about the diameter of a Red Bull can onto one of the wooden fence posts, but it came undone right away. Sirvent fumed. "Here I am the new guy and Tony's on the flybridge and he's yelling at me: 'You're embarrassing us.'" Chartier felt pressure, not just from the flybridge, but from all the people "waiting to jump on this boat and get the hell out of Manhattan." This time he wrapped the line around a post and doubled it back to the boat, securing the loop end to the stem bitt—the post on the front of the boat that's designed to receive docking lines. When Sirvent backed down, hard, the force yanked the railing right off—which had been his intention all along. He was clearing the way for people to board more safely.

Sirvent's boss, the Harbor Unit's operational supervisor, was already in South Cove when *Launch 9* arrived. Now he protested that pulling down the fences was destroying property. "Hey Sarge, did you look around?" replied Sirvent. "Everything's destroyed already." And the crew continued to pull out the railings so that people boarding could step easily from the wooden ramps onto the bows of the boats—ferries, water taxis, and other vessels—converging on the scene.

"Once we did that we had people just streaming onto the boat," said NYPD Officer Tyrone Powell, on duty that day as the boat's navigator. "These dust-caked people, they were ready to go," he recalled. "Now we had like Noah's Ark. . . . We had everybody on that boat. We had animals. We had babies without parents. Everybody was covered in soot."

"They were handing us little children," confirmed Chartier. At first he was confused: *Where's the mother and father?* Later he learned that a nearby daycare center had been evacuated. "We took everybody. As many people as we possibly could fit onto the boat. . . . Ty and I actually tied down somebody in a wheelchair on the front." They set the wheelchair carrying a man, in his sixties, "more disabled than old," on the bow near the anchor and secured it to a handrail with ropes.

"Dogs, cats, everything came on this boat," said Powell. "That's why I call it Noah's Ark."

Sirvent worried about the nannies in particular. It bothered him that dozens of empty strollers had been abandoned along the water's edge after crew from other boats wouldn't permit them aboard. "I was thinking: *Wait a minute. They've got a two-year-old or one-year-old. They're only the nanny. They've got to tell people that they're somewhere in another state with their child and there's no phone service.*" So he instructed his crew to stow the strollers in the vessel's skiffs and then offload them with the passengers on the Jersey side.

---

Florence Fox didn't have a stroller. Just a four-year-old clinging to her, growing increasingly distressed. When Fox spotted the police boat, she decided it was her ticket to safety and rushed down to the water's edge. "You have to take me," she pleaded with the officers on board. "Look at her. I have a child." It's hard to say for sure, because no one was taking notes, but the launch she boarded may well have been Sirvent's *Harbor Charlie*.

After passing Kitten across, Fox boarded herself, stepping her bare feet down a winding stairwell to a small bunkroom. There sat another woman, tall and blond, holding a six- or eight-month-old baby. The baby was quiet, and the mother was too. Fox asked the woman if she had a cell phone. She wanted so much to call Kitten's mother to let her know they were safe. "I think she's the one that told me there's no service." Beyond that the two didn't speak.

It didn't take long for the boat to cross the river. Fox, who had never before been in New Jersey, found herself at a big office building among a group of Manhattan refugees and people handing out bottled water. She asked someone for a cell phone but then discovered that she couldn't recall Silverton's phone number. She had known the number by heart. But now, as would happen to so many people in shock that morning, she couldn't retrieve it.

She recognized several nannies from Battery Park. One held a baby about six months old. "She was just crying and the baby was crying and she was crying. I told her, 'You know, you have to take care of the baby. Look at the baby.'" Fox decided she couldn't stay there. "I didn't want Kitten to be subjected to that," she explained. Change in the little girl was already apparent in her expression and behavior. "I knew she was going to come out traumatized, and if I could save a little bit of that . . . Everything that I did I was thinking about Kitten." So she rinsed their hands and faces and started walking. *I'm going to find a hotel.* Carrying no wallet, and therefore no money or identification, Fox intended to call upon the kindness of the desk clerk. "I just wanted a room where I can wash Kitten, give her a bath, give her something to eat." As she walked, she asked residents for directions.

---

Time and time again, Sirvent and his crew maneuvered the police launch into South Cove to pick up passengers. "You know, God was with us, the maritime people," he said. What convinced him was how perfectly the tide lined up his bow with the wooden pier (now liberated of its railing) so that people could step easily onto the boat. The pilot and his crew proceeded to board around 100 people onto a boat rated to carry about 20. "We broke all kinds of Coast Guard regulations," Sirvent explained. "We had the cockpit full. We had people all on the outside deck. We had people actually sitting in the rowboat, the little skiff that was on top. Then we had people standing up in the flybridge with me."

Once every inch of usable space was occupied, Sirvent pulled away and headed due west, bound for an old ferry terminal in New Jersey's Liberty State Park. There, once again, a railing separated the water from the land. Passengers made their way over the metal gates and soon Sirvent backed the emptied launch out into the river. The Harbor Unit crew made 15 to 20 trips just like this. When clouds of dust left zero visibility, Sirvent switched on the radar and kept going, eyes red from the smoke, paper dust mask dangling around his neck.

As he pulled away from the ferry terminal after one trip, the pilot noticed that one of the passengers, a man in his forties carrying a tool bag that suggested he worked in some kind of construction, seemed to be examining the railing. Five minutes across, a few more for loading, and five minutes back. That was all the time the man had between Sirvent's trips across the river. But by the time the launch returned to the terminal, the railing had been disassembled and set off to the side so that the next load of people could just step off the boat. "This guy had the foresight to say, 'Hey, I have the ability. Let me take this time to help my fellow citizens by doing the right thing here.' And he did," That effort, that initiative, was "one of the little things" that Sirvent said has stuck with him.

During one of the police boat's many Hudson River crossings, Sirvent heard fighter jets roaring overhead. "When those [F-15s] were blowing down the Hudson River at about 400 miles an hour—I'm not saying I was crying because I don't cry, but—I had like tears in my eyes thinking about the might of this nation, and [that] there wasn't a damn thing that me or those jets could do to avoid this situation."

<hr/>

Although they couldn't stop the planes from crashing or buildings from falling, people from all quarters rose up and stepped forward to provide whatever assistance they could. All along New Jersey's North River waterfront, emergency medical technicians (EMTs) and paramedics, administrators and doctors, firefighters and police were working to establish and supply triage centers. Instrumental to their efforts were ordinary citizens helping every way they could. Personnel from nearby hospitals, medical centers, and emergency management offices worked with fire department and hazmat crews to establish makeshift facilities to decontaminate, assess, treat, and direct evacuees to different transit options. Their efforts were supported by the contributions made by employees of local businesses, among others.

One triage center was established directly across the river from the twin towers, in Jersey City's busy financial district just north of New York Waterway's Colgate Dock, off Paulus Hook. By about ten o'clock, the ad hoc treatment of injured people coming off the boats had become more organized. Soon, the waterfront plaza lay quilted with red, white, and yellow tarps. EMTs hovered, orbiting the injured who suffered from burns, breathing issues, broken bones, pelvic fractures, and lacerations, as well as emotional trauma.

Following mass casualty incident (MCI) protocols, the teams tagged patients based on the severity of their injuries. On victims with the most dire, yet survivable, injuries in need of the most urgent care, they used red tags. Yellow tags indicated patients in stable condition requiring hospital care but not in immediate grave danger. For the "walking wounded," and those with injuries so minor no doctor's care was necessary, they issued green or white tags, respectively. Black tags were reserved for the deceased and those unlikely to survive given available medical treatment. Later, a New Jersey EMS official would report that his group had triaged more than 1,000 patients in two hours based on how long it took for the team to exhaust the supply of triage tags they had stored in their specialized MCI response truck.

Medical teams caring for Manhattan refugees flooding off the boats marshaled all available resources. Adjacent to the waterfront plaza, now laid out with first aid supplies and equipment, was a fenced-off construction site with a trailer. Emergency personnel asked construction workers to help them gain access to the air-conditioned trailer for asthmatics and others with breathing troubles. Within minutes the fence was plucked up and removed. Meanwhile, businesspeople from the surrounding office complexes rolled out office chairs that could be used to wheel the nonambulatory. They ripped down Venetian blinds and piled up the slats for use as splints. They yanked all the commercial first aid kits off the walls and brought out stacks of them.

Beyond medical needs, evacuees were focused on calling and getting home. With most cell service down, communications presented a huge challenge until employees of a nearby computer company set up two folding tables and ran out phone lines so that people could contact loved ones. Other people working in the area brought out janitorial uniforms for people whose clothes had been burned or destroyed. When EMTs asked for water, a cola company sent two trucks filled with 64-ounce bottles. A pharmacy brought a pallet of saline solution for people to rinse their contact lenses. In this manner, individuals' efforts to help—even in the smallest of ways—made important contributions to the evacuation as a whole.

Among the patients treated at the triage center was Kenneth Summers, the Blue Cross employee who'd been hit by a fireball bursting through the elevators into the lobby of 1 World Trade Center. "He was all frontal burns," recalled Mickie Slattery, a paramedic from the critical care team that transported him from the waterfront to the Jersey City Medical Center. Later, he was moved to the burn center at Saint Barnabas Medical Center in Livingston, New Jersey, where he remained for three weeks, undergoing four skin graft operations to his arms and hands. Not until the end of September would Summers's wife and daughter inform him that his workplace, Tower One, had collapsed, along with its twin.

---

At around 10:15 A.M., Tammy Wiggs stood barefoot on the bow of fireboat *John D. McKean*, her clothes (including the mesh-backed Merrill Lynch jacket she'd never removed) dripping Hudson River water into the eight inches of ashy gray soot that blanketed the deck. She began coughing so violently that she vomited, and once the heaving started it wouldn't let up. Soon Karen Lacey, also barefoot and dripping, joined her on the bow. Quickly thereafter, the Marine Division crew dropped lines and headed out across the Hudson, anxious to deliver their passengers, several gravely injured, to one of the triage centers that had sprouted up along the Jersey shores.

Lacey was surprised to see people she knew on board, including several colleagues. She had no idea how they'd gotten here, but now, as the ragtag group headed across the river, everyone exchanged what information they had. Lacey learned that buildings in Washington, D.C., had been hit and that several other unidentified planes were still in the air.

In the crush of trying to cover events that were heretofore inconceivable, journalists had unwittingly amplified the panic by reporting multiple false rumors. These rumors spread over the airwaves to televisions and radios as well as via the Blackberry devices commonly carried in the days before smart phones. Throughout the morning, broadcasters warned that multiple airliners were unaccounted for. Fears of another hijacked jumbo jet prompted the military to scramble F-15s to the airspace over the capital with orders to shoot down potentially dangerous planes. One suspicious aircraft was subsequently revealed to be a medevac helicopter.

At 10:23 A.M., the Associated Press reported that a car bomb had exploded outside the State Department. A minute later, 1010 WINS radio station in New York City announced an explosion at the U.S. Supreme Court. These and other reports of terrorist attacks, later revealed to be false, heightened the already skyrocketing anxiety felt nationwide. All the way out in Bloomington, Minnesota, officials evacuated and closed the Mall of America. By 10:53, for the first time since the 1973 Yom Kippur War, Defense Secretary Donald Rumsfeld ordered the U.S. Armed Forces placed at defense readiness condition (DEFCON) 3.

Before that, at about 20 minutes past ten o'clock, *McKean* pilot Jim Campanelli was weighing possible docking options along the unfamiliar Jersey City shore-scape. At first he headed slightly north and west across the river, hoping to tie up at Harborside terminal. But when the 9.5-foot-draft boat ran aground in the eight-foot-deep channel, he backed out and headed south a quarter mile to another ferry landing at Paulus Hook, just south of the triage center.

Careful not to block the New York Waterway vessels offloading passengers at their regular berth, Campanelli pulled the *McKean* up to an adjacent dock. The current sucked the boat right against the dilapidated pier, making for a smooth landing. Though there were holes in the wood planking, the pier at least had functional bollards and cleats. The crew quickly made fast lines.

Marine engineer Parga was wrapping the bowline around a cleat on shore when he heard a horrified "Nooooooo!" erupt from the passengers on deck. He turned, still gripping the rope, to see the North Tower crumble, its antenna plunging straight down into the rolling dust.

From where she stood on the main deck of the *McKean*, Lacey had a clear, sickening view of the North Tower as it disintegrated before her eyes. "The first one was terror and fleeing," she recalled, "and the second one was, *Oh my God*. So many dead people. Just so many. I just couldn't even comprehend it. Now it wasn't personal safety, it was just sheer horror."

Wiggs, meanwhile, had been retching the whole way across the river. She was hanging over the side when a man interrupted her. "Ma'am, I know you probably don't want to be bothered right now," he began, "but for posterity's sake, I think you need to turn around." She raised her head to see the debris cloud mushrooming up. Not until some hours later would the notion of posterity become personal. That was when Wiggs discovered that the exterior columns that *Chelsea Screamer* Captain Sean Kennedy had watched slice through the corner of 3 World Financial Center had cut right through the section of the building where her sister worked.

Wiggs had dialed her sister Katherine "no short of 30 or 40 times" throughout her walk from the stock exchange to the Hudson. "Just hang up, dial again. Hang up, dial again." Sometimes she'd heard a busy signal, sometimes a recording announced that all circuits were busy. Katherine, eight days shy of her twenty-sixth birthday and 18 days away from her wedding, had fled quickly after the planes hit, but later returned to retrieve the bag she'd left under her desk containing the bridal undergarments she needed for a gown fitting scheduled later that day. *My mom's gonna kill me if I don't have these*, Katherine thought. Bag in hand, she managed to escape the building, again, and walk north to her apartment on the Upper East Side.

But Wiggs's college roommate had not been so lucky. The young woman, who had only begun working on the North Tower's eighty-ninth floor a short time earlier, perished. "The man who had me turn around," said Wiggs, "had me watching the building that killed my roommate."

Fireboat *McKean*'s crew, meanwhile, had just witnessed the deaths of hundreds of brother firefighters—friends and colleagues whose lives had flickered out in an instant. They were desperate to get back to the site. But first the crew had to offload passengers and cut through the two fences that stood between the evacuees and their deliverance.

To firefighters on the job, barriers to entry are little more than an everyday complication. Spotting the fences, marine engineer Parga grabbed a Halligan bar (a multipurpose forcible entry tool with an adze and pick end) and a gas-powered Partner saw. He summoned firefighter Tom Sullivan to help him cut holes through which the evacuees could reach the plaza—and, beyond it, the relative Avalon of Jersey City. While the *McKean* crew gnawed through the fences from the water side, Jersey police officers and firefighters chipped away from the land side. Soon they created openings big enough for both the ambulatory and the disabled.

As he had been doing since he first leapt aboard the fireboat, telecommunications specialist Rich Varela, shirtless, tattoos visible on his chest and arms, was helping fellow passengers. He was boosting less mobile people up and over the *McKean*'s cap rail onto the dock when he spotted a familiar face. The man whose lower leg had shattered when he jumped onto the stern deck was being transported off the boat in a chair. Varela thought he recognized him. *Was that the security guard who told us to leave the area beneath the pedestrian bridge?* Lending a hand to help lift the chair over the side, Varela felt a wave of gratitude that the man had convinced them to leave when he did.

When Lacey finally had her feet planted on the pier, she gave the man in the bunker pants and thick glasses, whose name she never learned, one last thank you. He reached out his arms and pulled her in for a bear hug. All she could think about, as she braced herself for the long walk home to Hoboken with no wallet, no keys, and no shoes, was that these firefighters were going back there. "Their mission had just gotten so much worse."

Varela harbored the same concern. When he heard the collective gasp that accompanied the crumbling of the North Tower he began to doubt that he would make it through the day. *All right,* he said to himself. *This could be it, man. This could be the last day of New York as we know it.* And then he thought of those firefighters on the boat.

They were frantic to offload passengers so they could return to the smoking ruins. "Our guys are there," Varela recalled them saying. "That's when I turned to Tom. I remember saying to him, 'I'm coming with you. You guys need help.' In my mind, I thought they were gonna be like, *No fucking way. You're not coming.*"

Instead, Sullivan said, "Let's go."

So Varela jumped back aboard fireboat *McKean,* joined by two other civilians, a Wall Streeter who yanked off his suit jacket and button-down before climbing aboard and an older gentleman who explained: "My son's in that building."

During the short trip across the river toward the wreckage, Varela's thoughts wavered between contemplating the dead and reconciling himself to the concept that this day might be his last. "It really felt like, *I might die today* . . . And I was okay with it." *These guys need help,* he thought. And that was it.

People fled to the water's edge, running until they ran out of land. © U.S. Coast Guard, photo by Brandon Brewer

Evacuees cluster along the waterfront just outside the fence surrounding the Coast Guard office building at the Battery, where Port Authority Commerce Director Richard Larrabee sought refuge after being caught in the first collapse. © U.S. Coast Guard, photo by Brandon Brewer

Fireboat *John D. McKean* carries evacuees to Jersey City. Passengers and crew aboard include Karen Lacey, Tammy Wiggs, Rich Varela, Bob Nussberger, Tom Sullivan, Gulmar Parga, and Jim Campanelli. © Ron Jeffers

Passengers disembark just north of Paulus Hook in Jersey City. A ferry terminal receives smaller ferryboats and NYPD vessels, while larger boats, including fireboat *John D. McKean,* drop their passengers at the abandoned wooden pier on the left. On the shore, EMTs have begun laying out color-coded tarps to tend to the injured in their makeshift triage center.

Liberty State Park ferries and NYPD police boats pick up evacuees in South Cove.

Fireboat *John D. McKean* pumps water at the foot of Albany Street after its return to Manhattan, having dropped passengers at the Jersey City triage.

This aerial view, facing north, shows North Cove on the top left. Fireboat *John D. McKean* is tied up at the seawall at the foot of Albany Street. Farther south, NYPD launches and other vessels can be seen nosing in to rescue evacuees at South Cove.

The view south from Manhattan shows tugs racing from Staten Island and New Jersey to the Battery. On the left is the southern tip of Governors Island. The Verrazano-Narrows Bridge is visible in the background.

Tugboats nose up to the seawall along the southern tip of Manhattan to evacuate passengers.

Hornbeck Offshore Transportation's ocean-going tug *Sea Service* becomes a makeshift ferry. Not since the earliest days of the tug industry were the same vessels used for both passenger ferrying and towing. © Capt. Mike Littlefield

A bedsheet announces Hoboken as the destination, and evacuees board by ladder across the bow of Moran Towing Corp. tug *Turecamo Boys*. © U.S. Coast Guard, photo by Brandon Brewer

Fireboat *John J. Harvey* can be seen loading passengers just south of South Cove, adjacent to the Museum of Jewish Heritage. Farther south, New York Waterway ferries and tugboats load passengers from the seawall in Robert F. Wagner Jr. Park as a U.S. Coast Guard vessel approaches.

The view north from above Governor's Island shows smoke-filled Lower Manhattan and the Battery at the southern tip of Manhattan. New Jersey is on the left.

Long lines for Circle Line, World Yacht, and New York Waterway boats at 38th St. on Manhattan's West Side extend for more than 30 blocks. Some wait for three hours to board a boat. © 2001 New York City Police Department.

New York Waterway ferries and tour boat *Chelsea Screamer* (far right) evacuate passengers as the second tower collapses. The white tent covering the World Financial Center ferry terminal, where Pete Johansen has been helping to load passengers and dock builder Paul Amico is about to disembark, can be seen at the edge of the advancing dust cloud. Amico will soon establish a makeshift ferry terminal at the Downtown Boathouse pier (on the far left). © 2001 New York City Police Department.

New York Waterway boats nose up to the seawall at Robert F. Wagner Jr. Park, north of Pier A (with the peaked roofed tower). Just out of view is the small dock where *Chelsea Screamer* Captain Sean Kennedy asked firefighters to break the lock so passengers can board.

Staten Island Ferry captains, including James Parese, make runs back and forth to Manhattan all day, evacuating more than 50,000 people.

The view southeast from above smoke-filled Lower Manhattan shows North Cove at the bottom center. Just south of North Cove, retired FDNY fireboat *John J. Harvey* has already begun pumping, as evidenced by the white spray pouring out from the boat's deck monitors. Farther south, active-duty fireboat *John D. McKean* is tied up at the seawall off Albany Street. Still farther south other workboats have nosed up to the seawall to receive passengers.

Still caked in dust, VIP Yacht Cruises' dinner boat *Excalibur*, with Captain Jerry Grandinetti at the helm, evacuates passengers from the Downtown Heliport. © Capt. Mike Littlefield

Moran Towing Corp. tug *Margaret Moran* delivers people from Manhattan across the East River. Red Hook Container Terminal's shipping cranes are visible in the background. © Capt. Mike Littlefield

This aerial view, facing south, shows the West Side Highway along the Hudson River. The World Financial Center and Battery Park City emerge as the prevailing winds push the smoke and debris cloud to the east.

CHAPTER **8**

# *"A sea of boats"*

"HELPLESSNESS." THAT WAS the feeling consuming Lieutenant Michael Day on his approach to Manhattan shortly after both towers fell. Drawing closer to the smoke-choked Battery, he peered through binoculars at a foreign landscape. Lower Manhattan had become an achromatic world churning with dust and paper. The snow-like, debris-clogged gray air contrasted with the blue sky beyond the smoke. "You'd look behind you and it was a beautiful day. The weather was incredible," Day recalled. "And then looking at Manhattan . . ."

Desperate, ashy people—stacked 10 deep, maybe more—pressed up against the railings along the water's edge. Though "a sea of boats" had already rallied—tugs, tenders, ferries, and more, pushing into slips and against the seawall to rescue as many as they could—Day could tell that more boats were needed. Now, just before 10:45 A.M., the Coast Guard formalized the rescue work already under way by officially calling for a full-scale evacuation of Lower Manhattan.

"All available boats," Day began, issuing his first of many VHF marine-radio broadcasts summoning backup, "this is the United States Coast Guard aboard the pilot boat *New York*. Anyone wanting to help with the evacuation of Lower Manhattan report to Governors Island."

Back at Activities New York on Staten Island, the VTS had been issuing its own calls for mariners to respond. But Day said he never heard them. Clogged radio channels combined with the loss of one of the Coast Guard's main antennas from the top of 2 World Trade Center had left Day unable to reach his command.

straight lines that would provide the shortest distance between two points. By 10:15 A.M., people flooding north on foot from Lower Manhattan started piling up at Pier 84, at the foot of West Forty-second Street, prompting the company to begin shuttling passengers—600 at a time, aboard its three largest tour boats—on continuous trips across the Hudson to Weehawken. Word spread that the company was offering free passage to New Jersey, and by midday aerial photographs showed thousands of people standing in lines that continued for more than 30 blocks, from the West Fifties south to West Twenty-third Street. Some waited for three hours to board a boat. By nightfall, six Circle Line boats had transported about 30,000 people.

---

Once Hanchrow learned that Circle Line was already moving passengers, he dialed a friend at the company to talk through logistics. It seemed to Hanchrow that Lincoln Harbor, located about a mile across the river in Weehawken, New Jersey—a straight shot northwest from Chelsea Piers—was the best drop-off option. So, shortly after the second tower came down, the Spirit Cruises captains launched their own shuttle service from Pier 61 to Lincoln Harbor with Hanchrow at the helm of the *Spirit of New Jersey* while his colleagues captained the 145-foot *Spirit of the Hudson* and the 192-foot *Spirit of New York*. Deckhands aboard the three boats used clickers to make sure they stuck to their certified capacities: 600 on *New York*, 575 on *New Jersey*, and 425 on *Hudson*. "It didn't make sense to go over capacity," explained fellow Spirit Captain Daniel Scarnecchia. "What would we have done, got there 10 minutes quicker? The gain wasn't going to overpower the potential loss." As the Chelsea Piers guards and auxiliary police helped funnel foot traffic to the pier, the boats loaded up and dropped lines for their first seven-minute runs across the river.

Next the captains had to figure out how to tie up safely without use of their usual docking equipment or facilities. While the other boats made their way toward the harbor's breakwater, Hanchrow hoped to dock at "a tiny spot" along the south side of the seawall.

Upon his approach he discovered that it was occupied by a Rein-auer tug. He watched as an evacuee crawled her way to land, rung by rung, across a horizontal ladder suspended over the water from the tug to the seawall. This was hardly a safe maneuver, nor an efficient way to offload passengers. Having put in plenty of years as a tug captain, working for Reinauer among other companies, Hanchrow didn't hesitate before picking up the radio mic to bark out orders at the tug's captain. "Dude, you've gotta get that fuck-ing thing outta there."

"We're doing what we have to do to evacuate people," the cap-tain responded.

"You've got 12 people on that boat and they can't get off because of your fendering," said Hanchrow. "Get that fucking thing out of there. I've got 600 people I'm going to get off in 10 minutes. It's taking you five minutes to get one person off. You've gotta move. Nose up to me and get your people on my boat." And so the captain did.

Then Hanchrow set about docking the 175-foot vessel at a spot that "looks like a postage stamp when you're trying to land the *Spirit of New Jersey* on it." The gangway they'd brought with them was too long for the narrow section of seawall, so crew mem-bers scouted out another shorter section from the assortment that different charter operators stored there. Hanchrow radioed his friend, VIP Yacht Cruises Captain Dennis Miano, to ask if he knew whose gangway it was. "Just take it." So Hanchrow and his crew rigged it to be able to disembark passengers from the main deck cargo door. Their plan worked well, at least until the tide went out.

Even if they weren't quite accustomed to ferry duty, the Spirit Cruises captains were certainly in the habit of carrying passen-gers. Unlike at the Battery where proximity to the tower collapses and the resultant smoke and debris conditions caused outright panic, the people who'd stepped into long lines winding through the parking lot between Pier 62 and Pier 63 remained orderly. Even at its peak, when the lines ran up the West Side, people stayed calm, just grateful for a ride home. Each time the three dinner boats loaded 1,600 passengers and set back out across the Hudson it was clear that they were making a dent. By day's end the Spirit Cruises vessels had delivered approximately 8,000 people off Manhattan Island.

***

Lincoln Harbor Yacht Club's general manager, Gerard Rokosz, couldn't stand there any longer watching the towers burn. Seconds after the first plane hit, he'd heard the call that sailboat *Ventura* Captain Pat Harris had made to the Coast Guard. He'd looked out the window of the club's corner office to see fire licking out from the north face of Tower One. After the second plane hit he'd stared, like everyone around him, at the rolling smoke until he "got tired of looking at it and hearing all the chatter on the radio." He contacted the Coast Guard to share the best resource he had to offer: "We have a pier if you need it."

Not long after, he received a call from someone at Circle Line asking if its boats could disembark passengers at his marina. Rokosz granted permission. With the arrival of the first Circle Line boat minutes later, and the first Spirit Cruises dinner boats not long thereafter, Lincoln Harbor's evacuation depot service had begun.

The Lincoln Harbor dockmaster, meanwhile, had been scrambling to get to the marina from Bayonne since he'd heard about the second plane. That Tuesday was Janer Vazquez's day off, but even the street closures that prevented him from getting to Lincoln Harbor by car didn't deter him from heading in. He'd driven as far as his mother's place, on the Bayonne–Jersey City border, where he grabbed his nephew's bike. Then the five-foot-11-inch-tall, 41-year-old man pedaled the child-sized bike two miles to Liberty Landing, where he knew a friend of a friend who had a boat. The boat owner agreed to run Vazquez the four miles upriver to his workplace in his 27-foot Sea Ray, but before they reached the mouth of the Morris Canal a Coast Guard patrol boat halted them.

Once Vazquez explained that his boss, Rokosz, had called him in to help with the evacuation efforts the Coast Guard personnel escorted the Sea Ray to the marina. Vazquez arrived just as the first boat pulled in. For hours thereafter he scurried back and forth along the 500-foot dock making fast and letting go lines and helping people disembark as boat after boat dropped its passengers.

Evacuees arrived by the thousands, many of them with no clear sense of where to go next. The managers of the nearby Academy Bus Company, however, recognized that they had access to an essential resource for facilitating a waterborne evacuation. Rokosz received a call: we've got buses trying to get over to you but the roads are closed. So Rokosz called the Weehawken Police Department and spoke with a sergeant he knew. Before long Academy buses were shuttling thousands of people from the marina to either the Hoboken train station or Giants Stadium, a centrally located landmark from which people could arrange a pickup or other transportation. The flood of evacuees reminded Rokosz of "the retreat from Stalingrad." They wanted to know where the buses were taking them, he recalled: "'New Jersey,' I told them. 'It's not that big a state . . . You're not far from anything here. We'll get you home. Someone will pick you up. We're taking you to the stadium. Call somebody and get picked up.'"

———— ⟨⟩ ————

Soon after passengers began lining up to await Spirit boat transport, the hundreds of people in queue in the parking lot just north of Chelsea Piers became thousands. Seeing the crowds swell, the operator of a neighboring pier stepped up to offer his own docking facility for use in the evacuation.

Back in the 1980s, when Manhattan's western shore was deemed a wretched, fetid eyesore rather than valuable frontage, an electrical contractor from Seattle named John Krevey had gone looking for a cheap place to set up shop. He'd wound up renting space in a dirty, rat-infested paper warehouse adjacent to the all-but-abandoned Chelsea Piers. Back in Seattle, waterfront property had always been the most expensive. It struck Krevey as odd that here "in the great Port of New York" riverside real estate was the cheapest. Such was the harbor's state of decline. The no-man's-land along the water's edge allowed a bit of freewheeling on Krevey's part. Recognizing the potential of the small stretch of shoreline behind the warehouse, he decided to expand his empire.

So, maximizing the 40 feet of frontage included in his lease, Krevey cleverly docked the short end of a 360-foot-long rectangular barge at the water's edge, thereby extending his domain a full 14,400 square feet into the Hudson River. Having installed the barge—a former car float once used to transport cargo-laden freight cars across the Hudson from New Jersey for offloading— he dubbed it Pier 63 Maritime, a public-access pier that quickly became an unparalleled "old salt" destination. A New York City attraction with no hint of a "touristy" feel, the barge soon became a tiki bar/restaurant/arts space. The scrappy little Shangri-La, where visitors could watch a performance, take in a sunset, learn to paddle a kayak or outrigger canoe, explore historic boats, hop on a dinner cruise, or dance away a warm summer night, appealed to gritty boat people and young partiers alike.

On September 11, Pier 63 Maritime called out like a beacon, drawing countless mariners and community members to this outpost that had come to feel like a home. The magnetic pull to this spot helped galvanize a critical component of the maritime evacuation by offering another route off the island. After all, a successful evacuation depends on docks as well as boats.

From a motorboat on the Hudson, Krevey had watched as the South Tower spewed a torrent of soot that smothered his Battery Park City neighborhood. Then he headed north to the foot of West Twenty-third Street. As the boat traveled upriver, Krevey watched throngs of anguished, ashy people surge up the West Side Highway. He wondered how he could help.

Back at Pier 63 Maritime, he spoke by phone to the operators of the 600-passenger boat *Horizon*, which had previously scheduled a charter to depart from the pier at two o'clock that afternoon. "I talked to them about possibly being involved in a relief effort to get some of the people out," Krevey recalled. Soon enough, "they pulled in and we started forming lines." He quickly set his plan in motion, transforming the pier and the parking lot into a makeshift ferry terminal.

"Bruce, I need you." When retired administrative project manager for the Metropolitan Transportation Authority, and Pier 63 regular, Bruce Rosenkrantz arrived shortly before 11 A.M., Krevey immediately put him to work.

"You've got me," Rosenkrantz replied, relieved to be given a job—some concrete task to perform in the midst of all this havoc. He set out for the parking lot on his assigned mission, but when he registered the masses of people in the long lines, he faltered. *I don't want to cause a stampede*, thought Rosenkrantz, before returning to Krevey to voice his concerns.

This time Krevey escorted him back out with what was, Rosenkrantz explained, a "perfect Krevey" solution: a roll of red paper tickets. They spotted an auxiliary police officer, handed him the roll, and asked him to distribute the tickets to people needing a ride across the river to New Jersey so they could begin forming a new line. Bifurcating the river of evacuees eager to get off the island, Krevey had created a distributary channel—another way out.

Soon more Pier 63 regulars arrived—many of whom had headed there instinctively, drawn by the sense of the pier as a sanctuary. Among them was John Doswell, a waterfront consultant and maritime event producer, who quickly set to work helping to mold the lines into switchbacks so that more people could occupy the limited footprint of the parking lot in front of Basketball City. Accustomed to organizing people waiting to party, not evacuate, Doswell, Krevey, and other volunteers nevertheless applied their crowd-control skills to this new situation. They rigged up blue ropes tied to white plastic lawn chairs to organize the line. Krevey stepped among the people, holding his favorite megaphone up to his lips so he could answer individuals' questions for the benefit of all within earshot.

---

By happenstance, the subway train that former Fiduciary staffer Bonnie Aldinger had hurtled herself into in the wake of the second impact was an uptown train. That determined the course of the rest of her day. Instead of heading home to Brooklyn, she stepped off at Twenty-third Street, where she knew of a diner with a television. There, over a glass of orange juice that she hoped would cool her nerves, news reports filled in the blanks about the fate betiding her former colleagues on the North Tower's ninety-seventh floor.

She also learned that the bridges and tunnels connecting Manhattan Island to the rest of the world were being shut down. With home no longer an easy option, Aldinger set out for the next best place: the public-access pier that *felt* like home, Pier 63. In the wake of her layoff, she'd spent much of the summer paddling with the Manhattan Kayak Company, where she was both an instructor and a partner. The relief she felt every time she eased her boat out from the slip and left the city behind had kept her in New York despite losing her job.

Now, as she crossed the West Side Highway into the familiar territory of the parking lot leading up to the pier, Aldinger kept her focus straight ahead. She couldn't bear to look downtown at the smoke rolling from the towers. She hiked up a set of steep wooden stairs, unlocked the Manhattan Kayak Company office, and sent an e-mail message to her parents: *I'm okay. Details later.* Back downstairs, she was comforted by friends' familiar faces. Among them was John Krevey's wife, pier co-owner Angela Krevey. Aldinger was standing with her when her friend's face went white, her hand rising to cover her open mouth. It was 9:58 A.M. Aldinger spun around to see that all that remained of the 1,362-foot-high building that had been her workplace two months prior was a column of thick gray dust.

There was nothing Aldinger could do for her coworkers, but she could help the people around her. She opened up the kayak company office to passersby in need of working phones or water and then she joined in evacuation efforts on the pier. Three party boats would soon begin a free ferry service, circling back and forth to New Jersey. One of those boats was the VIP Yacht Cruises vessel *Royal Princess*, captained by Dennis Miano and crewed by the *Ventura*'s captain, Pat Harris.

After an unsuccessful attempt to fuel up his sailing yacht at a Morris Canal filling station and an aborted effort to rescue people from the seawall just north of the Battery with Jerry Grandinetti, Harris had decided to find a safe place for his existing passengers: the mate and his family. The timing of that decision led to what Harris singled out as "one of the great moments of the day."

Earlier that morning, as Harris explained it, the mother of *Ventura's* mate Josh Hammitt had been on a shuttle bus headed to Newark Liberty International Airport when she'd spotted the burning towers. Worried about her family, who lived so close by in Gateway Plaza, she'd gotten off the bus and hitchhiked her way back east, winding up on the waterfront of Liberty State Park. She had been looking out over the Hudson at smoke and debris blowing across her apartment building, worrying that her children might be caught in the middle of it, when suddenly the *Ventura* pulled into Morris Canal with her family on board. "She just dropped to her knees," recalled Harris. "You could see a mother's relief flooding out of her."

Harris had just finished making fast the *Ventura's* docking lines in a marina there when a man pulled up alongside the boat in a hard-bottom inflatable dinghy. He was diabetic, the man explained. Did they have any sugar? Welcomed aboard, the man hoisted himself over the side and asked to stay. Harris agreed and in turn requested permission to use the man's boat to cross back to Manhattan.

"I got a first aid kit, a bunch of towels, threw them in the dinghy," Harris explained. "I had to go to the other side to see what I could do." Wearing his NYPD safety vest and Harbor Unit Auxiliary hat, Harris set out for North Cove. "Halfway across the Hudson in this little tiny rubber boat I got this feeling like, *This is a very vulnerable position.*" Before him the notch of waterfront that he called home lay dust-cloaked and swirling with smoke and debris. Did he really want to go back? *Am I going to do any good over there?* he wondered. *What's the use of this little first aid kit and these hand towels in the midst of all that?*

By now the Hudson was choppy, the river swarming with vessels. All their wake action left Harris bobbing about, feeling "very, very small." For the first time since he'd watched a jet slice through the North Tower, Harris let his guard down. "I didn't have anybody around me to be responsible for," he explained. "I felt vulnerable and not like I had to be in command and take charge." *Do I really want to do this?* he wondered. "But of course there was never any doubt." As Harris saw it, the situation that morning was "every mariner's best case and worst case scenario. . . . It's a horrible situation. *And* you're able to help."

Then the helmsman on a small Coast Guard boat spotted him. The boat sped over on high alert. But when the crew spotted Harris's NYPD garb, the boat slowed and they waved him along. "That waving me on put me over the edge at full speed ahead," Harris explained. "There was a little transfer from one mind to another that: We're on the same team. Let's all go in there and do something!" He steered the dinghy straight to the *Ventura's* regular North Cove berth, a few floating docks away from where Grandinetti had pulled away in the *Excalibur,* which was now ferrying passengers and supplies back and forth around the harbor.

When Harris stepped onto the wooden dock, his feet sank several inches into the gray-white powder that coated every surface, every leaf on every tree, "like a heavy snowfall." Above him, long reams of flaming computer paper glowing orange corkscrewed about the air.

Heading up the ramp that led to the plaza, he spotted "somebody military" with a rifle. By nightfall, 750 National Guard troops would be stationed in the city. By morning that number would climb to 3,500. Then Harris noticed VIP Yacht Cruises owner Bob Haywood Sr. standing by the *Royal Princess.* "Can you help us get this boat out of here?" Hayward asked Harris. "I remember looking around and saying there's nothing I can do here, but I can certainly help there." So he stepped aboard.

Just then, recalled Harris, two bewildered tourists appeared on the scene, one German, the other from Ecuador. "They were kind of stunned, wandering around totally out of place and completely disoriented." They too boarded the *Royal Princess,* joining Harris and Captain Dennis Miano at the helm. The four of them became the ad hoc crew of the 125-foot, 200-passenger dinner yacht. Harris's first challenge was to excavate the ropes securing the boat to the pier. "I had to dig down past my elbows just to find the docklines, getting all that dust in my face, in my lungs, coughing and kind of digging through."

Captain Miano backed the boat from the slip and steered north. Finished with his decking duties, Harris made for the bridge, but to do so he had to cross through blizzard conditions on the open upper deck. The grayish-white powder lofted by the head wind engulfed him. "I remember saying to myself, *This is bad shit. You can't breathe this.*" But of course to continue aiding in the evacuation there was no avoiding it. Like hundreds of thousands of others, Harris took in lungfuls of toxic power, the true cost of which would only become apparent years later. In the moment, although he had some sense of the potential danger, Harris knew there was only one thing to do: keep moving forward.

When Harris reached the wheelhouse, he was covered in so much dust he was scarcely recognizable. Miano, meanwhile, had heard over the marine radio that people were queued up at Pier 63. We're going to take them across to New Jersey, he told Harris. Harris didn't think twice. Participation was "instinctive," he explained. "It was right place, right time . . . It was just the right thing to do." But he had no intention of breathing in more of that dust than he had to. Down in the dining room, where tiny blocks of safety glass from a broken exterior door or window lay sprinkled across the dark, patterned carpet, Harris grabbed a white tablecloth off one of the neatly arrayed tables and tied a section of it across his face.

It must have been about noon when the *Royal Princess* pulled up to Pier 63, recalled Harris. As Miano maneuvered the boat into docking position Harris readied the lines and took in the scene before him. He spotted John Krevey "doing crowd control" at his "little emporium." There must have been thousands of people there, recalled Harris. Krevey "had everybody queued up in a long snake like you would have in the velvet ropes. . . . He had everybody organized and flowing onto the boats. Somehow he put that all together." The crowd watched their approach. "We pulled up port-side-to," Harris recounted. "That's the side that had the broken glass. There was still all this dust all around you by the bulwarks and in the corners, and I probably looked like a snowman, as somebody called me later."

A voice called up from the crowd: Where the hell has this boat been?

From the wheelhouse Miano responded. "This boat was at Ground Zero."

It was the first time Harris heard the designation that later would become so iconic, so inextricably linked with the World Trade Center site.

Captain Miano gave Harris a clicker, instructing him to stop at 300 passengers, though the boat was only certified for 200. "We were going to be safe *and* bend the law," Harris explained years later. "He's a pro, I'm a pro. We both know that stability is built on a number of factors and we could push that limit and get these people out of there."

He was struck by how people's patience and the organized queues created a sense of calm in the midst of chaos. "Everything was beautifully ordered and when the boat was full, they just said okay and we pulled out," Harris recalled. Despite being a captain himself, Harris had stepped easily into a support role. "I was just along for the ride and part of the team," he said. The captain "gives the orders and you just say, 'Yes sir.' It worked out very, very nicely."

The German tourist had taken to his ferry deckhand role as well, employing what Harris called "good German efficiency." The gangway—more of a three-foot-wide plank with no handrails—extended from a lower deck at midship to the pier and Harris worked the boat end while the tourist stood by the end on the pier. "I remember him moving one arm in a circle and the other pointing just like a policeman would," recalled Harris. "And then on the Weehawken side we did the same thing," emptying the boat of passengers, level by level.

The *Royal Princess* looped into rotation with the Spirit Cruises and Circle Line boats dropping off in Lincoln Harbor. With each run, the organization on the New Jersey side escalated visibly. Among the boats "there seemed to be a natural pattern evolving," Harris said, ". . . a counterclockwise motion of flow outbound to New Jersey." Captain Miano ran the boat at a regular cruising speed of about six knots and, by Harris's recollection, the round trip took about 15 minutes. Though plenty of people boarding were dusty and disheveled, nobody was injured and just one woman, crying hysterically, was distraught enough to require extra care. Mostly, they were incredibly grateful, Harris recalled.

"There was a proud moment, and I often get choked up when people ask me or I think about it," said Harris.

> "That moment when we're disembarking people, I would say at least a third paused for a moment at the top of that gangplank and put their hand on my forearm and said, 'Thank you. Thank you for helping us out.' And I remember looking at their faces and seeing jaw lines that were set. Eyes that looked determined. And I thought, *This is a culture that we can be proud of.* There was cooperation. There was no panic. There was a realization that we'd been hit hard, knocked down, got back up, and we were determined to get through this. And I thought, *This is New York. This is America.* It was basically at the worst of times that we rose to the occasion. The horror of people's parts and the debris—that has less of an impression on me than the positive. I was seeing the paradox in humanity—the best of our kind at one of our darkest moments. That will choke me up more than the horror."

That day the *Royal Princess* made five or six round trips between Pier 63 and Weehawken, transporting as many as 1,800 people off Manhattan Island.

———⊗⊗⊗———

Just before the first tower came down, Pamela Hepburn had helped to evacuate children from a school in Lower Manhattan where she'd been working as a polling-place volunteer during the morning's election. After taking shelter in the school during the collapse, she'd slogged her way to the waterfront through the ankle-deep layer of gray powder and mangled paper blanketing the streets to borrow a bicycle that she figured would be the fastest way to reach her nine-year-old daughter, Alice, who was in middle school on Twenty-first Street between First and Second Avenues. Once Hepburn had collected Alice, she'd focused on finding somewhere to be, somewhere safe, where the air was clean. Their loft apartment on Murray Street, four blocks north of the trade center site, was out of the question. Who knew what condition it was in now? A tugboat captain who'd been working in New York harbor for more than two decades, she made a beeline for Pier 63. "That's where we hung out so much," she explained years later. "My little compass needle went right there."

At the pier she encountered friends, including Angela Krevey and several other mothers who were trying to busy their kids. Alice joined the other children, and Hepburn set out to help with the evacuation. The lines at Pier 63 were growing. Although her 1907 tugboat was currently out of service and under restoration, Hepburn also owned a whaleboat called *Baleen*—a 26-foot-long, Navy-issue, open motorboat traditionally used as a lifeboat, in rescue operations, or to transport personnel between vessels or to shore. *Baleen*, currently berthed downtown at Pier 25, was what Hepburn had available, so she biked south, secured the boat and a longtime acquaintance to help crew it, then returned north.

Back at Pier 63, she discovered that the big charter and dinner-cruise boats now making loops across the Hudson were all delivering passengers to Weehawken. "I thought, geez, there have got to be people who live in Jersey City," Hepburn recalled. She decided to evacuate people farther south. She spotted Bruce Rosenkrantz and asked him to find people who needed passage to the Jersey City–Hoboken City line. She could take 14 or 15 passengers, but warned that they might get a little wet.

At the foot of Twenty-third Street, two lines now serpentined around the parking lot. One line was for passengers boarding boats from Chelsea Piers. The other was for people boarding from Pier 63 Maritime. Among the thousands waiting were Chris Reetz and Chris Ryan, the sales associates from L90 on Twenty-third Street, now caught up in the general evacuation of the island and looking for a way home. Ryan scanned the crowd for familiar faces. And then it began to sink in. A lot of people had just died. He started going through his mental Rolodex thinking, *Who do I know that was down there?*

A man with a megaphone—John Krevey—was calling out directions, instructing people about which line to join. People continued to swarm to the waterfront, yet the lines remained orderly, with no shoving or cutting. As each boat arrived, crews loaded up passengers to capacity, and beyond.

Reetz and Ryan stepped into the Pier 63 line for boats heading directly across the Hudson to Weehawken, planning to hoof it to Hoboken once they reached the Jersey side. The line moved faster than they expected, but still they waited for close to two hours before reaching the front. Then someone—Bruce Rosenkrantz—yelled out, "Does anyone want to go to Hoboken?"

"We do!" they replied, thankful for the promise of a direct route home.

"I would have gotten on an inflatable boat," explained Reetz years later. "I would have gotten into a canoe or a kayak just to get off that island." And Pamela Hepburn exuded confidence. Reetz and Ryan were among the passengers who boarded the whaleboat for that first run. As soon as they boarded, Reetz let out a sigh. *I'm on a boat. I'm safe. These people are getting me to Hoboken.* He'd had no hesitation about climbing into this small boat rather than one of the larger passenger vessels.

Ryan, too, was struck by Hepburn's commanding presence, which was reinforced by the declaration by her acquaintance, now crew member, who proclaimed to passengers, "Pamela is one of the best tugboat captains in the harbor. She's been running tugs for more than 25 years." *She's been doing her job as long as I've been alive,* thought Ryan.

*Baleen* was weighed down, sitting low in the water—"gunwales to," as Hepburn expressed it—when she steered it out into the choppy Hudson. As the boat headed south, water splashed up over the sides. No one on board said a word. To this day Ryan recalls that Hepburn "was clear when all of us were fuzzy. . . . She was bringing me to safety and she made me feel safe while doing it regardless of all the crazy shit that was going on."

When Reetz saw the sunny, clear skies over New Jersey he felt a wave of relief. He was off the island, out of harm's way. It occurred to him that this was his first time on the Hudson River, and he dipped his left hand into the cool, salty water. When he looked up he saw downtown Manhattan engulfed in smoke. He thought of the destruction, the chaos, the death. The juxtaposition of the two skies—the blue sky on the right and the black sky on the left—overwhelmed him. *It's a shame*, he thought, *that my first time on the Hudson is on a beautiful day—like this.*

Hepburn had wanted to transport her passengers farther south along the Jersey waterfront, but docking *Baleen* posed specific challenges. Her goal was to serve the most people by making multiple quick trips across the river, but she needed a tie-up site that could accommodate a boat that rode so low in the water. Through the years she'd spent working in the harbor, Hepburn had been trained to look at the shoreline as a resource to help deal with all sorts of issues: "loss of power, beaching the boar, or putting a line out to get beer." In this case she needed a spot where passengers could disembark safely. Local knowledge pointed her to Long Slip, an old, narrow pier with railroad tracks located at the Jersey City–Hoboken line. She didn't expect to be greeted by police when she arrived.

Long Slip was by no means an official drop-off point. As Hepburn steered her whaleboat toward the pier, Ryan, who had worked on boats when he was younger, could tell that this would not be the easiest landing. The pier was nothing more than a raised slab of concrete with rocks jutting out at the waterline, and Hepburn nosed in with no fendering to cushion the impact. Ryan heard a crunch as the boat made contact and it occurred to him that this captain was risking damage to her boat in order to ferry them home.

In an instant, uniformed police pounced. They ordered the boat away, saying that no one could get off. Hepburn didn't flinch. "Excuse me," she said firmly. "We've got people on here who've just walked to Twenty-third Street from the World Trade Center. They need to disembark." That was enough. Her crewmate was already wrapping the bowline around a spike that stuck out of the concrete.

"We were like friggin' refugees," recalled Ryan. "And she was a leader." When the police backed off and began helping, Ryan was struck by how they had succumbed to her authority. "She did that with her confidence and her clarity." Instead of blocking their path the police helped people out of the boat and up the rocky ledge.

Next the passengers faced decontamination. The Hoboken Fire Department hazmat team, under the direction of the Hoboken health officer Frank Sasso, who was concerned about the potential of a chemical or biological attack, had established a makeshift decontamination facility, building a giant shower out of PVC piping and in-line spray-heads fed by three fire engines. More than 10,000 people were decontaminated that day.

Nearby St. Mary's Hospital had set up a field hospital unit where more than 2,000 people were ultimately triaged. Unlike at the triage center just north of the Colgate Dock, most of those arriving in Hoboken were uninjured. According to EMS reports, only 179 patients required hospital transport, and most did not need medical care.

Reetz recalled being surveyed for injuries, sent through a sprinkler system of sorts, then doused with water by a firefighter cracking open a fire hose. Reetz might have wound up soaking wet, but at least he was safe in New Jersey, not far from his apartment. Now his head swam with a mix of relief and disbelief. *What the hell just happened? What do we do now?*

All across the country, people were asking those very same questions, but not all with the same level of urgency as those caught up directly in the aftermath of destruction, including those still working in New York harbor.

# PART THREE

⊷⊷⊷

# THE AFTERMATH

I dream'd in a dream, I saw a city invincible to the
Attacks of the whole of the rest of the earth;
I dream'd that was the new City of Friends
—Walt Whitman

# CHAPTER 10

# "We *have to tell us what to do.*"

ALL MORNING NEW YORK WATERWAY'S PORT CAPTAIN, Michael McPhillips, had been fielding questions. NYPD Harbor Unit officers, Port Authority representatives, and captains from a handful of different tug companies, among others, contacted McPhillips for information and sometimes direction. Usually his job involved tracking vessel schedules, managing captains and deckhands, vessel maintenance, and Coast Guard compliance. Being thrust into this position of responsibility out of scale with his position overwhelmed him. When a tug captain called asking where he should pick up and drop off passengers, McPhillips mistakenly sent him to a pier with nowhere near enough water to accommodate such a deep-draft vessel. "I caught it before they got in there, but it would have ripped out the bottom of their boat," he recalled. "It sucked, honestly. I had all these other boats calling that were coming in to help and I had to make all these decisions."

Given McPhillips's prominence on the radio, it made sense that when Coast Guard leadership arrived on scene shortly after the second tower fell, an officer contacted him by VHF. "He asked what was going on. I explained it to him," McPhillips said. "I asked if I could go over capacity. He responded with a 'yes'. Then he asked if we needed help. And I said, 'Absolutely.'" A short while later, McPhillips heard the VHF radio broadcast calling for "all available boats" to aid in the evacuation.

Though neither can say for certain, the Coast Guard officer who called McPhillips that morning may well have been Lieutenant Michael Day aboard the Sandy Hook Pilot boat *New York*. After the boat had dropped marine inspectors at strategic points along the Battery to help guide evacuees toward boats and prevent vessel overloading, it continued its long, slow "barrier patrol" along the tip of Manhattan, swooping around from the Hudson to the East River and back again.

The goal was visibility. Not only did this sweep afford the personnel aboard the pilot boat good vantage points for looking up both sides of Manhattan to watch for points of traffic congestion or other issues, it also made the boat itself, with the U.S. Coast Guard ensign waving, more conspicuous. Day sought to empower mariners with the idea that the Coast Guard was on scene, present, and available.

From his post in the wheelhouse as the boat moved up the East River, Day watched a ferry pull off Pier 11 carrying a boatload of passengers. A great cheer erupted as the boat backed away. Day found it strange to see people so happy to leave Manhattan, though he only needed to shift his gaze slightly to see the smoke and be reminded why.

Despite the efforts of the inspectors, Day saw vessels precariously loading far more passengers than they were designed to carry. Some mariners even radioed to *tell* him that they were carrying more people than permitted. They weren't so much asking for permission as reporting the fact, Day recalled. While witnessing botched Haitian and Cuban migrations on overloaded boats earlier in his career, Day had seen the horrors of drowning refugees clawing for capsized vessels. Now he felt torn. "We were trying to get as many people off the island as we could," he said. But, he acknowledged, "If a boat flipped over we'd have even more people in the water because of my actions. And I was responsible. I felt responsible."

Like McPhillips, who couldn't reach his supervisors, Day was making on-the-fly decisions that normally would have been beyond his authority. When mariners requested permission to violate regulations, Day explained, "I rogered, laughing at myself a little bit. It was just like, *wow! I broke more rules than probably I've enforced in my whole Coast Guard career.*" He later joked that at the time he'd reassured himself with the thought, *I'm just a lieutenant. What are they gonna do to me?* In truth, making leadership calls normally left to those at "flag level" weighed on him.

But Day's rule breaking was far from reckless. Like many other mariners who took a more flexible approach to compliance that morning, Day made considered decisions in response to unprecedented circumstances. As disaster researchers James Kendra and Tricia Wachtendorf point out in their book *American Dunkirk: The Waterborne Evacuation of Manhattan on 9/11*, "Just because rules were broken does not mean that there was a lack of order, organization, or concern for safety." Instead, rules were being:

> "thoughtfully disregarded, even in the desperation of those first hours when people just wanted to do *anything*. We call this *rule breaking with vigilance*. Everyone broke the rules, but they broke them gracefully, with sensitivity for consequences and with a sure-footed sweep through a potential minefield of possible mistakes and accidents."

Crucially, the violations still reflected the guiding principle behind the rules—"Taking positive action to make things better," as Day described it. And the infractions arose in direct response to extraordinary conditions. "It got easier to break them as time went on," Day explained. "I won't say it didn't matter . . . But you know what? They're looking at a burning hole. It didn't really matter in the balance of it." Ultimately, Day did his best to encourage captains to act safely while continuing to summon additional boats in hopes that more vessels on the scene might reduce the impulse to overload.

Part of what gave Day the confidence to make on-the-fly judgment calls was the leadership style espoused by his commanders, Captain Harris and Admiral Bennis, which emphasized encouraging their people to take the initiative to make their own decisions. "I really felt when I worked for Admiral Bennis that I was totally empowered to do the right thing," explained Day. "Do the right thing and I'll take care of you. Don't worry about it. I mean as long as you can say this is why and the reason."

"I'm a huge believer in empowerment," Bennis affirmed in an interview with a Coast Guard historian months after the attacks. His longstanding leadership style had been to encourage his team to "go out and make magic and be brilliant." His approach on September

11, once he finally made it back to New York at about 3 o'clock that afternoon, was no different. "What I did is what I always do. I went in with the folks. I sat down with them. I got a briefing—the first of thousands of briefings. I asked very few questions—some pointed questions just to be sure we're going on the right track," Bennis explained. "I had a team that I had complete trust in, and I let them know that right up front. . . . I just tried to stay there in the midst of them, but, absolutely, I never micromanaged them."

In fact, that approach had actually trickled down to Bennis and Harris themselves from the highest ranks of the Coast Guard. From his earliest communications with his superiors following the attacks, Bennis was reassured that he and his team would be trusted to do what needed to be done. "They were all pretty confident with our abilities and capabilities," he explained of his higher-ups, who were located all across the Northeast.

> "I knew what I wanted to do. I knew from working with the city the best way to accomplish it. . . . But I wanted to know, was I in fact a free agent? And I was. As the commandant put it out later, he said he allowed his field commanders to let their creative juices flow and do what they needed to do, and I was able to do that."

Instead of establishing a top-down command and control structure, the Coast Guard, from the top brass down to the on-scene rank and file, allowed for the organic, needs-driven, decentralized response that played an enormous role in the ultimate success of the boat lift. This approach, in turn, allowed mariners to take direct action, applying their workaday skills to these singular circumstances, without being stifled by red tape.

As Kendra and Wachtendorf explain: "Even with an eye for security and safety, [Coast Guard officials] were still able to recognize the value of an improvised citizen response to the terrorist attack." Instead of interfering with the waterborne evacuation that was already under way, the Coast Guard *participated*. Commanding officers, both on- and off-scene, granted their blessing, legitimizing the spontaneous, unplanned evacuation through facilitation and support, thereby encouraging more mariners to get involved.

No one had foreseen the sudden need for evacuating a huge swath of Manhattan Island. Yet as terrorized people continued to flee to the waterfront, more and more boats turned up to rescue them. To Harris the white wakes visible in aerial views over Lower Manhattan looked "like the spokes of a wagon wheel." Mariners were already responding. "Nobody had to be told to help," Harris explained. "The asking, basically all that did was put people on the right frequency. People were already primed."

As greater numbers of vessels and evacuees amassed along the shoreline, streamlining operations became the biggest challenge. By midmorning, so many mariners had joined in the effort that the regular passenger piers jammed up with boat traffic, thwarting the vessels most suited for using those piers from efficient operations. "The only way to fix it was to get organized," said Harris. That organization was implemented in large part by Day and the pilots operating aboard the *New York*, which continued its barrier patrol. Their efforts were made easier by the relationships that both the Coast Guard and the Sandy Hook Pilots had with the New York harbor community.

Day's initial broadcasts from the helm of the pilot boat set the tone for the Coast Guard's position of cooperation and participation rather than interference with or controlling the efforts already under way. "United States Coast Guard aboard the pilot boat *New York*," Day began. "All mariners, we appreciate your assistance." Rather than ordering people around, he and most of his Coast Guard and pilot colleagues did their best to leverage their existing relationships with members of the New York harbor community to foster a team approach.

"The New York maritime public probably responds better to someone they know than someone they don't," Day explained. "New York as a city and the maritime community in particular, is built on relationships." Day's history of "externally focused" work within the Coast Guard, including the year he'd spent in an "industry training" exchange program, helped him have more engagement with the community than a typical Coast Guard officer.

In 1998, he had worked with the Port Authority in 1 World Trade Center, meeting with maritime industry people to learn about the impacts that Coast Guard regulations and actions had on commerce. He had also been working with the Harbor Operations Committee, which held regular meetings bringing the Coast Guard together with commercial operators, the Sandy Hook Pilots, the Port Authority, the Army Corps of Engineers, and other harbor stakeholders to "seek nonregulatory solutions" to port problems. "I was in a unique position to understand relationships between the Coast Guard and the public," Day explained. "As a result of it I had a degree of trust."

What struck Day that morning, and stuck with him thereafter, was what he called the "clarity of purpose: hey, we're doing a good thing to help people." Helping others "is a core ethos of the maritime community," he explained. "It's just part of the culture.... You're at sea and someone needs your help and you'll divert hundreds of miles out of your way to help someone."

Day also recognized that the Coast Guard's regulatory functions and role as "enforcers" could end up as a divisive force if not carefully managed. Day was mindful about fostering "a unity of effort," as the guiding principle of operations that day. One choice that helped serve that approach was the decision to join forces with the Sandy Hook Pilots and use their boat as a floating command center. By nature of being a law enforcement and regulatory agency, the Coast Guard would, of course, have some clashes with boaters during a normal day. The pilots' daily operations, however, routinely included more exclusively collaborative relationships with other harbor operators.

Harris explained the success of the evacuation's collaborative approach this way:

> [Day] "had a really good relationship with the maritime industry in the port. But it wasn't just him. Also on that boat was Andrew McGovern.

Andrew was recognized, had a lot of personal leadership power. Between the two of them, it became conversations. Nobody demanded anything. Nobody yelled at anybody. Nobody ordered people to do things. Everybody said what they wanted to do and the guys on the *New York*, the pilot vessel, made it possible for them to do it. They could talk to them. They knew them. They had sat through meetings with them for years.

---

Aboard the *Chelsea Screamer*, Captain Sean Kennedy didn't count heads. Instead, he and crewmate Greg Freitas focused on loading as many people onto the 56-passenger thrill-ride speedboat as they could, as fast as they could. "We filled it up. If we peaked it, it was by only a few." And then the captain shot straight across the Hudson to the closest New Jersey dock: at Liberty Landing in Morris Canal. As passengers disembarked, Kennedy took a few empty water bottles and filled them from a hose on the pier. He wanted to be able to offer water for people to wash their hands and faces, to clear their mouths and throats.

On his second run, Kennedy headed toward a cluster of people in Battery Park who walked clutching clothing to their faces. They'd gathered four blocks south of the World Trade Center near Pier A, a historic municipal pier built in 1886 that had stood vacant since 1992. Kennedy called out to a firefighter on land there, asking him to cut the lock on the gate that prevented people from reaching the water's edge. Seeing the gate opened, people scrambled toward the boat.

After Kennedy had offloaded more passengers back in New Jersey, the camera crew that had originally chartered the boat as a platform for shooting footage earlier that morning told him they needed to submit tape to their office near Rockefeller Center. Could he run them back to Manhattan anywhere near there? Kennedy said he could drop them off at a pier near West Forty-sixth Street. Hearing this, some passengers asked if they, too, could disembark there instead of New Jersey.

As he set up to land on a barge at the south side of the *Intrepid*, the aircraft carrier that's now part of a sea, air, and space museum, Kennedy saw mobs of people queued up to board Circle Line and World Yacht boats from a nearby pier. He spotted a man waving and trying to get his attention and sent his crewmate Freitas to run over and ask what the man wanted. The man was looking for a way to cut the line. He offered $4,000 cash if the *Screamer* would deliver him and three others across the river now. But Freitas refused. "That's how desperate people were to leave immediately," Kennedy explained. "Money didn't matter."

---

Already off the island, Karen Lacey had no money. And no shoes. When she stepped onto the abandoned pier in Jersey City, the Merrill Lynch director was numb, but not with cold. Although her clothes were soaked through with Hudson River water, here on the Jersey side the sun shone bright, warm, and unobscured. "I was thinking about shoes," recalled Lacey, "about having to take a fairly long walk without them." Her Hoboken apartment stood about two miles to the north, but Lacey planned to make a stop along the way. "We'll stop at Modell's and get sneakers," she told Tammy Wiggs. Although Lacey, having finally dropped her bag in the river, was without a wallet, she couldn't imagine the store clerks, seeing her wet and gray, would turn her away. "They'll give us shoes just to get to Hoboken and I'll come back and pay for them later," she figured.

As the two women walked through the streets, Wiggs barefoot and Lacey in shredded stockings, people couldn't help but notice them. For the most part they were "gracious, not gawking," Lacey remembered, though she did overhear a few whispers: 'Oh my God. They were *down* there.'

Dozens of passersby offered their help: 'Do you need water? I have shoes. I can give them to you. We'll go upstairs. We'll get it for you. We'll be right down.' But, spurred on by the promise of a shower, Wiggs and Lacey refused the overtures and kept walking.

Twenty minutes into their journey, they reached Modell's only to find it shuttered behind metal security screens. "That's when it hit me," Lacey explained. *It's 10:30 in the morning; Modell's isn't open.* Consumed by shock, panic, and the instinct to flee, her mind had circumscribed the morning's events as some "uniquely New York thing." She'd somehow imagined that once she got across the river "people were going to be having lunch and selling shoes." Realizing that the store had sent home its employees on a Tuesday morning somehow cemented for Lacey the gravity of the World Trade Center attacks. There was nothing to do but continue on.

The superintendent of her building on Hudson Street in Hoboken unlocked the door to her sixth floor apartment. As she pulled together some clothes for her young colleague to borrow, Lacey asked herself which would be the least offensive, cleanest looking pair of panties she could loan, then chose a pair of purple Calvin Kleins.

"I never thought I'd wear someone else's underwear," said Wiggs.

"I never thought I would offer them," Lacey replied. "But they're there if you want 'em."

A black ring marked the tub after they each finished showering. No matter how many times Lacey blew her nose, what came out was gray.

Wiggs felt like she had "little glass shards" in her eyes. She had no lens solution available, yet was so desperate to wear her contacts so she could see that she swished the lenses around in her mouth in an effort to clean them.

When Lacey's family came by the apartment, Wiggs hid in a back room. She declined Lacey's offer to join them when they went out to eat at a local restaurant. Instead she used Lacey's landline to call everyone she knew, and finally connected with a friend who offered to drive her to her parents' home in Baltimore.

---

Also walking barefoot through Jersey City was Florence Fox, still carrying four-year-old Kitten, who peppered her nanny with questions. "Where are we going? When are we going to get there?" Fox enlisted her help with the search. "We have to look," she told the frightened girl. "Kitten, can you see anything? Can you see something that looks like a hotel?" The little girl had grown calmer but Fox could tell she was still scared by the way that she clung. That fear would end up affecting the child for years to come. "I was talking to her just to make sure she was okay."

They eventually found a hotel. The lobby was mobbed with people trying to book rooms, but none of the others were covered in dust. Fox strode to the front of the line. "Maybe it was arrogant, but I really didn't care." "Can I get a room?" she asked. "They must have thought I was crazy." The clerk was sympathetic but couldn't help. Every single room was booked. Throughout the area, people left stranded by the closures of the region's three major airports were hauling their luggage through the streets— some hitchhiking, some pushing commandeered airport luggage carts—on the hunt for buses, rental cars, and hotel rooms.

Eyes burning, skin itching, and barefoot, Fox had carried Kate through the streets only to end up at a hotel with no vacancies. As she begged, then argued with the desk clerk to no avail, a few hotel guests, in town on business, offered to take them in. They showed Fox to a room, then left the two alone to get cleaned up.

Fox washed Kate first. The girl was shaking. Instead of drawing her a bath, Fox stood Kate in the tub, letting the shower water run so she wouldn't have to sit in the stew of toxins that rolled off her body. Once the little one was clean and wrapped in a towel, Fox prepared to bathe herself. "You can sit on the floor," she told Kate, then climbed in and closed the shower curtain. Kate screamed.

"Don't close the shower curtain!"

"I don't want you to get wet."

"I don't care if I get wet," the girl pleaded. Fox looked at the frightened child and saw that she was changed. *She's right*, Fox thought. *After what we've been through what is water?* So she showered with the curtain open.

Once they were both clean, Fox distracted Kate with cartoons and picked up the phone. She still couldn't retrieve her employer's phone number. Instead she dialed her sister whom Fox knew could reach the girl's mother.

Then the girl and her nanny curled up on the bed to wait. "I just remember feeling so scared. And feeling cold. And looking at Kitten and being so afraid for this child." The people who'd taken them in brought food, but Fox doesn't remember eating. She doesn't remember exactly what happened next.

———⊗⊗⊗———

Although Kitten remained separated from her parents for nearly 12 hours during the frightening ordeal of fleeing her home, her bond with Fox, who loved the girl like the two were family, offered her safe haven throughout. While finding trust and comfort among perfect strangers was one of the hallmarks of the disaster, the solace of familial ties could not be underestimated.

Shortly after the first tower fell, beginning law student Gina LaPlaca had aligned her fate with the men who'd saved her from stumbling down the subway station stairs. But now, temporarily blind, eyes bandaged in a Manhattan hospital, she decided she needed to be with family. When somebody finally managed to reach her mother on the phone, the frantic and relieved woman arranged to have LaPlaca's uncle, John Coyle, who worked near East Thirty-third Street, pick up her daughter in the hospital. The two men waited with LaPlaca until he arrived, and then it was time to say thank-yous, swap phone numbers, and issue heartfelt (yet ultimately unrealized) promises that they'd all keep in touch.

LaPlaca found great relief in being taken under her uncle's wing. Coyle, who had helped raise LaPlaca after the death of her father, signed her out of the hospital and explained the facts of the situation: "Your neighborhood's off limits. They're not letting anyone in there. They're evacuating everybody. You're gonna go home with me to Staten Island." With that he hooked his arm in hers and pointed them toward the Staten Island Ferry, three miles to the southwest.

But first they stopped at a street vendor to buy some large-framed "Jackie O" sunglasses. Not only was LaPlaca feeling self-conscious about her bandages, any hint of light that made it through the dressings irritated her injured eyes. For an hour the young woman was guided, unseeing, through her new city. She registered the shifts between neighborhoods by sounds and smells. Chinatown struck her as particularly loud and full of activity. Then, as the two proceeded farther downtown near the trade center, the streets went quiet. "You would hear sirens but there weren't really cars on the street, or the usual activities there," she recalled. Walking "as close to the water as we could," they crossed Wall Street, and soon enough LaPlaca arrived back where she'd started—where she'd wandered blindly through the dust cloud that morning. The smell caught in her throat. Now that she was in the care of her uncle, the weight of the day began to sink in.

The ferry terminal hummed with people. All morning James Parese and his fellow Staten Island Ferry captains had continued making runs back and forth to Manhattan, delivering more than 50,000 civilians off the island. On return trips from Staten Island, they transported emergency workers and supplies. Parese, who had started his workday at 5 A.M., wouldn't finish until 5 P.M.

Coyle weaved LaPlaca through the crowd to a spot to wait where they would be visible. In addition to a ferry, the two were waiting for LaPlaca's friend and houseguest who had undergone her own trials that day, wandering the Manhattan streets in ill-suited footwear and relying on the kindness of strangers. Through communicating with the friend's mother, LaPlaca's mother had coordinated the friends' reunion so that both young women would have a safe place to stay on Staten Island.

"There's a blond girl waving," said Coyle. "Is that her?"

The two friends embraced. "Thank God you're all right. What happened?"

"Oh my God. What happened to you?"

When they boarded the ferry, Coyle, "a creature of habit," shot straight for the same seats that he chose every day on his commute. All around LaPlaca heard the "whispered, small conversations" of shocked fellow passengers. Not until she was safe at the West Brighton, home of her uncle did LaPlaca notice her battered feet, all blistered and torn from her heeled sandals.

Wet as Chris Reetz, Chris Ryan, and Ryan's girlfriend were after the decontamination hose-down that greeted them in Hoboken, walking home made the most sense. But they all planned to meet up a little later. Reetz knew he needed some sort of support system—someone to rely on and someone with whom he could process all that had happened. "Chris," he explained, "was the closest thing I had to family."

McSwiggans Pub had become "a home away from home" for Ryan and his girlfriend. "We knew every bartender. We'd been to the owner's house. We knew his kids." So that was where the three went and waited for their fellow regulars to file in. "It was a weird kind of feeling in that bar," explained Ryan, an "uncomfortable happiness" about everyone who'd survived that revealed itself through nervous laughter. He recalled wanting to lighten the mood and then realizing that was not the right thing. "This was not a time to be funny. It's like telling a joke at a wake or something, and in many ways it was. I mean, holy shit. Everybody in there knew somebody who was dead or could have been dead. Or they didn't know yet if they were dead." And so the trio stayed late, sitting, and drinking, watching the television, and waiting for their friends to appear. Once they'd found this "stable place," they didn't want to go home.

---

For Rich Varela, home came as an afterthought. While Lacey reunited with family, Wiggs drummed up a way out of town, Fox secured a hotel room, LaPlaca headed for Staten Island, and Reetz and Ryan sought comfort in their neighborhood bar, Varela had remained at the post he'd been assigned by firefighters on the *John D. McKean*, which was actively pumping water to land-based engine companies. Varela doesn't recall what the *McKean* crew had asked him to do, exactly, but at the time he understood that his duty was to stay put. Before long it seemed like he was the only one left aboard. *What am I doing here?* he wondered, noting that while he stood wearing just a life vest everyone around him wore breathing apparatuses and protective gear. Still he didn't leave—not until a firefighter (maybe Tom Sullivan, maybe someone else) came back and asked, 'Why are you still here?' While the *McKean* crew would remain on station for days, the telecommunications specialist who'd volunteered his assistance was now free to go.

Relieved of duty, Varela immediately thought, *How the hell do I get out of here?* For the second time that day, he needed help getting off Manhattan Island. He walked north toward North Cove and stepped out atop the southern breakwater to scope out his options. Then a small, maybe 30-foot, aluminum boat pulled up, and a man called out over a loudspeaker.

"Hey, buddy. You all right? You need a lift?"

"Yeah."

"Where do you gotta go?"

"Jersey."

The guy nosed the boat in close enough that Varela could jump on.

Across the river, Varela stepped off the boat in the shadow of the Colgate Clock (the iconic 50-foot diameter octagonal clockface that had been overlooking the Hudson since 1924, when it stood atop the now-razed Colgate-Palmolive factory) and was greeted by triage center medics. They looked him over, gave him wet cloths to wipe himself off, and then directed him to the free buses that would deliver him to Newark Penn Station. Not until he settled into a seat on a New Jersey Transit Raritan line commuter railcar, at somewhere around three o'clock in the afternoon, did Varela process what he must look like wearing a life vest on the train. Neither the shock nor the generous purpose for which he'd sacrificed his shirt muted his embarrassment.

———— ⊶⊷ ————

By late afternoon, when crowds amassing along the shoreline began to dwindle, tugs, dinner boats, ferries, and other vessels shifted duties from delivering passengers *off* the island to ferrying emergency workers and others *onto* Manhattan as well as transporting goods. Throughout the evacuation and well into that first night people had sought to cross the river toward Manhattan as well as away. Some felt duty-bound because of their professions—firefighters, steel workers, doctors, nurses, journalists, and canine rescue squadrons among them. Others were desperate to find loved ones.

The Lincoln Harbor Yacht Club's general manager, Gerard Rokosz, fielded pleas from a man worried about his pregnant wife, fireboat *John D. McKean* transported a father concerned for his son, and New York Waterway captains reported denying passage to reporters. Coast Guard Boatswain Carlos Perez and his crew shuttled police officers; Spirit Cruises Operations Director Greg Hanchrow ferried fire department personnel, police, and "a lot of suits"; and on Jerry Grandinetti's first run back to Manhattan from Owl's Head, Brooklyn, he delivered medical personnel to North Cove.

The rescue efforts, meanwhile, demanded supplies. And like the evacuation, Coast Guard Lieutenant Michael Day explained, the supply runs "just kind of happened." The highly visible, 185-foot pilot boat waving a Coast Guard ensign provided a ready hub for rescue workers' requests. When firefighters approached asking for drinking water, Day and his colleagues made calls to the New Jersey Office of Emergency Management. Civilians on the Jersey side cleared store shelves, piling bottles along the waterfront. When Day radioed requests to mariners to run the supplies across the river he was inundated with volunteers. Rescuers needed dust masks and eyewash, wrenches and diesel fuel, and acetylene for torches to cut steel. Day and his team made requests to New Jersey and mariners delivered whatever could be gathered to their aid.

It was dusk when Day first stepped off the pilot boat *New York* into the "eerie gray snow" of Ground Zero. The mixed crew of Coast Guard and Sandy Hook Pilots personnel had established a good working relationship with emergency officials in New Jersey, and now Day was walking around the site, hoping to locate someone from New York City's Office of Emergency Management. "There were body parts everywhere," he recalled. The sight of a foot still in its shoe transfixed him. He couldn't take his eyes away. *This is a war. A siege,* he thought, eyeing the National Guardsmen patrolling the streets of Manhattan with M-16s.

Structural fires continued to rage around the World Trade Center site, orange glows penetrating the darkness left by power outages. The air hung thick with debris, the hovering dust spotlighted in the beams of the few construction light boxes that had so far been erected, courtesy of Weeks Marine. When the wind kicked up it lofted charred papers, sending them fluttering through the air.

———⊶∞⊷———

At last the message that nanny Florence Fox had sent through her sister reached Kitten's family. The four-year-old's mother was on her way. Silverton had been searching for her daughter since morning. As she sprinted from the townhouse to the nursery school and everywhere else she could think of to look, the towers came down around and on top of her, covering her with ashy gray soot. Only when firefighters warned her of a possible explosion and ordered her to board a boat did the distraught mother evacuate.

On the New Jersey side, Silverton ran into people she knew. She asked them if they'd seen Fox and Kitten. Little did she know she was closer now to her daughter than she'd been all day. Finally, at about eight o'clock that night, a call came through. Her daughter was safe, and not far away.

"I was expecting this almost fairytale reunion," recalled Silverton. "Kate would run into my arms and I would pick her up and swing her around. And then hug Florence. We'd all hug. And instead I got off the elevator and they were coming down the hall. Florence was carrying Kate. I'm not sure if Kate even recognized me." This was the first sign that Silverton, a psychologist, had of the post-traumatic stress disorder that would afflict the child in the days to come.

"We just cried and cried," recalled Fox.

———⊶∞⊷———

By three o'clock in the morning, Jerry Grandinetti had wound up less than 500 feet from where he'd started on the *Excalibur* that morning. All afternoon and evening Grandinetti had worked delivering evacuees off the island, transporting personnel around the harbor, and carrying supplies into North Cove. Many of the requests he'd answered came from the pilot boat, which was now tied up along the outside of the breakwater at the south end of

North Cove. Grandinetti had tied the *Excalibur* to the inside of that same breakwater. Still aboard were the two NYPD Harbor Unit officers who'd been assigned to help him. But not for long. In the predawn hours, a sergeant boarded.

"How are you guys doing?" Grandinetti recalled the sergeant asking the officers.

"We're good to go till daylight, Sarge."

"No you're not," their superior replied. "You're done."

Relieved of their posts, the officers left, and Grandinetti was suddenly alone with his thoughts. "I didn't know what to do then. I cracked a beer and sat in the wheelhouse. Then I decided, maybe I'd try to get upstairs to my apartment to close the windows and get my wife some clothes." He knew the two of them wouldn't be allowed home for a long while and this might be his best chance to collect some essentials.

With the power out, Grandinetti had no choice but to climb the stairs to the nineteenth floor by flashlight. Before he'd fled that morning he'd been hanging out a window with his camera. That window was still open when he returned, and now every object, every surface in his apartment was plastered with dust. He didn't stay long before heading back downstairs and retreating to the boat—the best refuge he now had.

Grandinetti sat in the wheelhouse. *What do we do now?* Despite his exhaustion he couldn't settle his mind. *I can't sleep,* he thought. *I can't sleep looking at this red glow.*

———— ∞∞∞ ————

*What the fuck just happened?* From the helm of the go-fast boat that he had commandeered that morning, Spirit Cruises Operations Director Greg Hanchrow tried to wrap his head around the events of the day.

All afternoon the Spirit Cruises dinner boats had ferried passengers from Pier 61 to Lincoln Harbor. Hanchrow and the *Spirit of New York* crew had to adjust their makeshift gangway system as the tide shifted, but still they managed to offload passengers safely and comfortably, down a ramp and through a main-deck cargo door. But by seven or eight o'clock that night all three Spirit boats were docked back at Pier 61. What had started that morning as a mission to rescue company assets by pulling vessels out of Manhattan had turned into a rescue mission for people, and ended with the boats secured back in their berths. By now it was getting dark, and Hanchrow had decided he'd better bring the boat that he'd appropriated back to Petersen's Boat Yard & Marina in Upper Nyack. Only a few lights shone at the trade center site where smoke continued rolling into the night sky.

Heading north up the Hudson River, his head swirling, Hanchrow looked over to his right at the West Side Highway. Suddenly it hit him. There were no cars. Instead a caravan of about 10 huge quarry earth-moving trucks with enormous tires lumbered south. *This is 12 hours later and we're already moving material*, he thought.

His next thought was: *I'm gonna have to figure out how to get down here tomorrow.*

When at last Hanchrow arrived home, emotion overwhelmed him. "I was sad, crying. I was mad. I'm very upset." He thought of his daughter. *Here I am in my nice cozy home with my daughter we've had for three months who's still speaking Bulgarian. Well, I'm glad I brought her to this country. Maybe she would have been better off over there.* With "a fucking big glass of rum" in hand, Hanchrow decided to push off some of the hard questions until later. *All these things are gonna have to be addressed at some point. But not now,* he thought. *There's shit that's gotta get done.* He might not yet know exactly *what* needed doing, but he was determined to make his way back onto Manhattan Island the next morning to figure it out.

In hindsight, Hanchrow called his plans to return "pragmatic." *I'm not in any danger,* he figured. *No one's shooting at me. There's nothing imminent.* Instead he felt a need "to go and be centered around the boats, around the pier, in the city saying, 'Okay, what are we gonna do?'" Despite all the day's uncertainties, Hanchrow was absolutely sure of one thing: "We need a time-out, and we need a huddle. . . . No one is going to tell us what to do so *we* have to tell us what to do."

CHAPTER **11**

# "Sell first, repent later."

AT DAYBREAK ON WEDNESDAY, SEPTEMBER 12, Sean Kennedy once again stood at the helm of his thrill ride tour boat *Chelsea Screamer*. With him were crew member Greg Freitas and more than a dozen National Guardsmen who had slept aboard another of Kennedy's boats, a dinner yacht called *Mariner III*. Kennedy had happened across the para-rescue specialists at about eleven o'clock the night before while they'd been preparing to set up camp outside at Chelsea Piers. When he'd offered better accommodations, they'd accepted, some settling into available cabins while others stretched out on deck, "still in their armor, guns by their sides."

Now it was dawn and, as promised, Kennedy was transporting them back to their duties. Smoke continued to roil up from the Pile—all that was left of the collapsed buildings—as he tied the boat at North Cove. The National Guardsmen climbed ashore and then set off between two buildings. Kennedy never saw them again. Just south of the cove, he spotted a friend, Huntley Gill of retired New York City fireboat *John J. Harvey*. Kennedy shuffled across the plaza to greet him, his feet disappearing beneath the ashy powder that reminded him of new fallen snow.

All night the fireboat had continued pumping, supplying river water to hose lines stretched inland. Chief Engineer Tim Ivory had barely slept in the hammock he'd strung up on the bow of the boat to ensure he could be called upon at a moment's notice. Several times he woke in a panic, fearing an air raid when U.S. fighter jets swooped low overhead. Gill, too, had slept fitfully, if at all, up in the wheelhouse. Now, as he and Kennedy spoke, Gill reached into the dust at his feet. "Look at that," he said, pulling out a card printed with the name "Windows on the World"—the famous restaurant that had occupied the top floors of the North Tower. Although little had yet been confirmed about the numbers and identities of the people who had been killed, it was already understood that, in all likelihood, the people in the restaurant when American Airlines Flight 11 hit had perished.

Having dropped off the National Guardsmen, Kennedy and Freitas decided to knock on doors to offer transport to anyone still in the area. Ultimately they evacuated about 20 people, many with pets, delivering them to Chelsea Piers.

Located directly up the Westside Highway from Lower Manhattan, Chelsea Piers facilities had served a major role in disaster response from the earliest hours of the attacks. By 11 A.M. on the eleventh, EMS triage centers that had been disrupted at the trade center site were relocated to sound stages at Chelsea Piers. A 160-bed trauma hospital was established in the studio space of the television show *Law & Order*, and ambulances from all over the region marshaled outside, awaiting dispatch. The piers offered water stations for people fleeing from downtown and became a key debarkation point for the waterborne evacuation, delivering more than 10,000 people off the island from its docks.

Then, the following day, more than 30,000 people arrived to volunteer their help and connect with other New Yorkers. Families of the missing gathered at the Chelsea Piers Field House and met with counselors. In the days that followed, thousands of uniformed personnel were fed in an events center at Pier 60, hundreds of rescuers slept and showered in Chelsea Piers facilities, and truckloads of donations and supplies were assembled and processed for delivery to the trade center site.

---

At North Cove, donations were stacking up. Supply runs had continued throughout the night, and the esplanade was quickly overrun. Just as they had for centuries, before containerization pushed shipping off the island toward Brooklyn and New Jersey, Manhattan's shores had become littered with break-bulk cargo—a wide variety of goods that had passed hand-to-hand onto vessels before being offloaded, also by hand, onto the dusty moonscape surrounding what would soon become known universally as Ground Zero.

"The supplies were coming in so fast and furious that we were running out of room and we couldn't distribute them fast enough," recalled Coast Guard Lieutenant Michael Day. By Wednesday, the flood of private citizens' donations had been supplemented with massive corporate contributions arriving in bulk. Mariners and land-based volunteers moved pallets of Levis, cat and dog food, galoshes, and flashlights—all manner of goods, some more useful than others. So many boats were pulling in to offload that the radios became useless for managing traffic in, out, and around North Cove. Instead a Coast Guard crew member assigned to the bow of the pilot boat used hand signals to direct vessel movements. "It was a hands-on VTS," explained Day. All this activity prompted discussions about where else boats might land supplies. As Day explained, the knowledge and experience of pilots and local tug captains helped immensely. Chelsea Piers and the Battery were identified and formally established as two additional supply depots.

Stacks of boxes and garbage bags full of donations covered more and more of the waterfront plaza around North Cove. John Doswell, the Pier 63 regular who had helped with crowd control during the evacuation, had hitched a ride aboard a small boat to fireboat *John J. Harvey*, where he was also a crew member, to offer what help he could. He and his wife, Jean Preece, wound up using a fire hose to clear an expanse of the plaza's hexagonal paving stones of the thick layer of dust that kicked up in the slightest breeze. Now at least donations could be kept slightly cleaner, and offloading would be easier.

---

Although Greg Hanchrow couldn't have predicted exactly what September 12 would require of him, he'd felt certain that a huddle was the best way to find out. So, first thing on Wednesday morning, at a coffee shop named Ruthie's just north of Pier 61, Hanchrow met with a handful of Spirit boat captains and other mariner friends to brainstorm.

"It's gotta be a disaster down there," said Hanchrow. "There's no place to stay, no place to sit. There's no water, no toilets, no phone lines." And what if there were more bombs? Wouldn't it be wise to station a "big evacuation device" nearby? Hanchrow called upon his old friend, Gene O'Hara, retired from the NYPD Harbor Unit, in hopes that he might help. "Is there any way we can get the *Spirit of New York* into North Cove?" he asked.

In less than 24 hours, the situation had changed entirely. While all manner of vessels had moved in and out of North Cove on the eleventh, helping with the evacuation, thereafter the FBI quickly took the lead in controlling the World Trade Center site and deciding who could come and go. "That's a tall order," replied O'Hara. But he offered to call his former colleague, Harbor Unit pilot Tony Sirvent.

Another mariner, Vince Graceffo, who had worked the deck aboard the *Spirit of New York* during the evacuation, chimed in to piggyback on Hanchrow's idea: What about food? Maybe they could feed the rescue workers, too? He said he knew a chef at the Tribeca Grill. Located in the "frozen zone" that had been shut down by authorities, the restaurant would be closed for the foreseeable future. (Soon officials would erect 12,000 feet of six-foot-high chain-link fence that would bisect the neighborhood called TriBeCa, for Triangle Below Canal, sealing off a zone patrolled by National Guardsmen wearing battle fatigues and helmets and carrying automatic weapons.) Maybe the managers would consider donating their fresh food that would otherwise go to waste. Then there was the well-stocked Spirit Cruises commissary. With the harbor closed and the country reeling, Spirit wouldn't be running lunch or dinner cruises anytime soon. The Spirit executive chef figured they had enough food to last at least a few days. *We could do this,* thought Hanchrow. They just had to secure permission.

A short time later, Sirvent nosed the bow of a police launch against the floating docks on the eastern edge of North Cove so that Hanchrow and O'Hara could jump off. Advised by Sirvent that there was a command post at the corner of Vesey and West Streets, Hanchrow and O'Hara trekked inland through the eerie landscape toward the heart of the disaster. As they walked past the green-domed 1 World Financial Center building, Hanchrow looked up at the trees and noticed a pair of pants dangling. *That's a fucking strange place for a pair of pants*, he thought. He surveyed the damage to the building whose whole first floor was blown apart and piled high with rubble. Looking up at the tree a second time, Hanchrow spotted what he hadn't registered at first: sticking out of the bottom of the pants were two feet. The sight was more than he could grasp.

The two kept walking, but geography was obscured by wreckage. Hanchrow kept shaking his head. *Unbelieveable. Unbelieveable.* "I didn't even know which direction to go." Finally they found a police chief who said approval for nonemergency services assets would have to come through the Jacob K. Javits Convention Center. The two would head there next. But first, they knew they'd best also secure permission to move the boat through the harbor.

Back on the waterfront, the Coast Guard flag flying atop the pilot boat *New York* offered some hope of answers. "All right, you're the cop guy, I'm the Coast Guard guy," Hanchrow told O'Hara. "Let's go see if the Coast Guard's there."

Hanchrow recognized pilot Andrew McGovern from the Harbor Ops meetings he'd attended, so he approached him first. McGovern steered Hanchrow to a Coast Guard officer. "Listen, we have the *Spirit of New York*, a dinner boat, and we'd like to bring it into North Cove and provide relief service here," petitioned Hanchrow. "We can feed 600 to 1,000 people an hour. The boat is geared and designed to have high turnover of people, and we don't have anything else to do."

The officer didn't say yes, but he did convey urgency, explaining that if Hanchrow had any intention of making this happen he'd better do so within the next 24 hours. As Hanchrow recalled it, the officer told him: "This is going to turn into something that you've never seen. Nothing's gonna come or go." Lower Manhattan was, after all, the site of a massive act of terrorism, and now formal structures for dealing with the aftermath were being pulled into place by multiple local and federal agencies. With that, Hanchrow and O'Hara headed back to the police launch for transport back to Chelsea Piers to work on setting the plan in motion.

Given all the transportation shutdowns, the easiest way for Hanchrow and O'Hara to get from West Twenty-third Street to the Javits Center at West Thirty-fourth was to walk. But they hit a roadblock at Thirty-third; the street was blocked by a tank and piles of sandbags. Blue-shirted cops were everywhere. *This is fucking crazy*, thought Hanchrow. The surreality didn't subside in the convention hall itself. Already, on the day after, thousands of people had gathered to offer up their particular skills and resources.

"I start getting in the line where the big boys are with the big toys," recounted Hanchrow. "There's this guy in front of me who's talking to all these white-shirt, suit people and he goes, 'I own an ironworking company and I got three trucks and 60 guys and they're parked in a parking lot outside the Lincoln Tunnel. You say the word and I've got 60 guys and welding machines and they're coming down the West Side Highway.' 'Okay, go talk to this guy,' they told him."

Next it was Hanchrow's turn to make his case. As he described his idea for a floating relief center that would offer shelter and food, as well as a mobile command post that could double as an evacuation vehicle, "their ears perked up." All right, you go talk to this guy, they told him. It sounded promising. But the next people he spoke with told him they'd get back to him and left it at that.

*What do you mean you'll get back to me?* thought Hanchrow. *What is this, a job interview?* More than "a little perplexed," he walked back down to Chelsea Piers.

Convinced that this was too good an idea not to execute, Hanchrow and O'Hara decided to move ahead regardless. O'Hara offered to call his girlfriend who used to know someone who worked for the governor. Hanchrow, meanwhile, called his boss. When the acting president for Spirit Cruises, who was working out of the Boston division, heard Hanchrow's plan for a four-day relief mission from Thursday through Sunday he replied that he'd watched the New York boats evacuating people on CNN. "Do whatever you need to do," Hanchrow recalled him saying. "You have my permission to use the assets any way you see fit."

The plan was taking shape. Spirit's chef loaded up food on the *Spirit of New York*. The boat crews loaded fuel from the *Spirit of New Jersey* to the *New York* in a completely unorthodox over-water transfer "with a big fucking Rube Goldberg kind of hose." Hanchrow scheduled Spirit crews to work round the clock. The *Spirit of New Jersey* would become a warehouse for donated supplies. "All during this time I'm like, *Of course this is gonna work*," Hanchrow said. "*It's a big boat. We've got a lot of food. We've got a lot of people. There's going to be a lot of need for all this down there.*" His guiding principle had come from his father, who'd always said: "Sell first, repent later."

⎯⎯⎯⎯⎯ ❧ ⎯⎯⎯⎯⎯

While Hanchrow and his team focused on the logistics of feeding rescuers, and Lieutenant Day and others helped usher supplies onto the site, the repercussions of shutting down the largest container port on North America's East Coast loomed large. Although the physical infrastructure of the Port of New York and New Jersey hadn't been directly affected beyond the destruction of the Port Authority headquarters in the North Tower, the whole harbor had been shut down, unleashing a ripple effect of serious commercial consequences.

Once he'd collected himself, after crawling out of the rubble of Tower Two and seeking refuge in the Coast Guard building at the Battery, the Port Authority's port commerce director, Richard Larrabee, had set to work reassembling his team and trying to get the port reopened. Not until he was safely inside, watching the North Tower fall on television, did the retired admiral fully grasp how narrowly he'd escaped being swallowed up by wreckage. He showered, changed into the spare Coast Guard jumpsuit that someone had given him, and then called his wife (who hadn't yet known his whereabouts) to tell her he was alive, but didn't know when he'd be home.

He caught a ride aboard a New Jersey police boat to the Port Newark waterfront and walked inland to a Port Authority administration building. Personnel there had suffered a clear, cross-harbor view of the unfolding disaster. "They were all just completely beside themselves," Larrabee recalled.

His first job was to track down his team. Remarkably, almost every one of the 100 people under Larrabee's direct supervision had made it out of 1 World Trade Center safely. (One man who had been attending a meeting in another part of the building did not survive.) Next, Larrabee would leverage his longstanding relationship with Rear Admiral Richard Bennis (at one time Larrabee had been his boss) to advocate for opening the port as swiftly and safely as possible.

The port commerce director spent the night at the Port Authority building, then early on September 12, he greeted one of his staffers, Bethann Rooney, who'd just returned by train from Washington, D.C., where she'd been speaking about homeland security, "before homeland security was the buzzword," as she explained years later. Rooney's boss hugged her, saying, "Thank God you're okay." Then he announced: "You're in charge of security."

Thus began her 14-year effort, first as security manager and later as general manager of port security, to create a security program "from nothing." "Security didn't exist in the maritime industry on 9/11," explained Rooney.

> "In terms of the Port Authority it was about crime prevention and loss prevention for cargo, and public safety-type matters. This was the same in every port around the country. Your piers, your docks were wide open. So on September 10, 2001, you could drive down to the port, take out your lawn chair, and sit down and have your sandwich and sunbathe at lunchtime right adjacent to the side of a ship unloading cars from Japan, completely open and accessible."

Big changes would be needed, both nationally and internationally. But here in New York harbor, the Port Authority and Coast Guard immediately aligned forces to find answers to some daunting questions. Later that morning, in a conference room in Port Newark, Admiral Bennis, Lieutenant Michael Day, numerous Port Authority police officers, Rooney, Larrabee, and others assembled to discuss what Rooney referred to as the new paradigm. "What is this thing called maritime security? The port is closed. When are we going to reopen it? How are we going to reopen it? What does that look like when we reopen it?"

On everyone's mind was the threat of more terrorist activity, recalled Larrabee. "The decision to close it was easy," he said. More difficult was "getting people to agree on the process by which you could reopen the port."

The Coast Guard was confronted with two opposing missions: protecting potential targets of a second-wave attack and continuing commerce in a port that regularly handled approximately 6,000 inbound and outbound containers daily, the closure of which created complications worldwide. The port shutdown prevented the movement of essential commodities that were crucial for running infrastructure—oil, gasoline, and aviation fuel—along with perishable goods like fresh fruit. Then (as now) the Port of New York and New Jersey was the nation's largest port for refined petroleum products. "Within 20 hours I was getting calls from the White House saying they're running out of gasoline in Portland, Maine," recalled Admiral Bennis. "New York is a huge petroleum port. Huge. We supply the petroleum to Logan Airport and all these other places, and people don't realize that."

Costs ran high, and both port and Coast Guard officials were keenly aware of the potential for longstanding economic damage resulting from the closure. "We operate in a very, very competitive world. If you ship goods from China," explained Larrabee, "you are looking for reliable, time-sensitive, low-cost factors to move your goods. You could send your goods through Los Angeles or Long Beach. You could send them through Norfolk or down through Halifax, or you could send them through Newark. The longer the port was closed, the less competitive we were, and the more likely it was that cargo could be getting shifted in other directions." Just as Commander Daniel Ronan had feared, the port shutdown would indeed cost $1 billion each day. The pressure was on.

Additional pressure stemmed from the transportation disruptions, some of which would continue over the long term, as well as the intense need for onloading and offloading supplies to and from the trade center site. The limitations of existing waterfront facilities were immediately apparent to people like dock builder Paul Amico whose expertise lay in creating bridges between water and land.

On the afternoon of the eleventh, even in the midst of helping to coordinate safe docking options and load passengers, Amico was already considering what infrastructure would be needed on the twelfth. He managed to get a message out to his shop to start building the hinge plates that he knew would be necessary to connect gangways to the shore. He knew he had a number of gangways in his yard, left over from use during OpSail 2000, and was sure he could find key places along the waterfront where they could be put to good use. "I knew we were going to have to put temporary facilities up to get supplies in, and ferry terminals to get civilians in and out."

One crucial first step toward building new waterfront access points was to identify conditions along the shoreline. This meant knowing what was underwater, out of sight at the water's edge. New York Waterway immediately made arrangements for a diver as well as a boat with a side scanner to map out, on September 12, the riverbottom terrain between the Holland Tunnel Ventilator at Spring Street and the northern edge of Battery Park City. They discovered that the area was littered with pilings that remained from the eight or so finger piers once existing there.

"A diver would come up and say, 'There's no way we could get a boat in there,' or, 'Yeah, we can get a boat in here,'" Amico recalled. This underwater reconnaissance would prove critical when, by Thursday evening, DonJon Marine began plucking moorings out of the riverbed to make way for Weeks Marine to come in with cranes and barges to begin loading out World Trade Center debris.

But before all that, at dusk on the night of the eleventh, Amico and the upper management of New York Waterway met at Pier 11 on the East River with representatives from New York City's Office of Emergency Management to discuss waterborne transport options. As Amico recalled, the basic message from the office to Waterway was: *Do what you guys do.* That meant something to the effect of: figure out how to move people from Point A to Point B over water. The questions that naturally followed included: *What docking facilities can we pull together? Where can we put them?* and *What boats are available?* Another meeting convened shortly thereafter at Waterway's headquarters in Weehawken to drill down to the specifics. "What we wanted to do was take a look at piers, pier heights, pier conditions, and what boats are available," recalled Amico. Waterway management jumped on the phone to call anyone who owned a fishing boat that might be used to shuttle passengers. And so the creation of an ad hoc system of ferries, terminals, and routes began.

With subway routes changed and the downtown PATH train tracks buried beneath World Trade Center rubble, ferries became a key mode of transportation from September 12 on. To compensate for disrupted downtown service, the PATH ran a free cross-river service uptown between Thirty-third Street and Newark and Hoboken, New Jersey. On September 13, the Port Authority reopened the Lincoln Tunnel, George Washington Bridge, and Port Authority Bus Terminal. But most subway stations south of Fourteenth Street remained closed.

City streets south of Canal Street weren't reopened to regular traffic until October 10 (and then only during certain hours). But businesses in other parts of the city began operating within days after the attacks. Indeed, some never closed. This being New York, city life and the commuting routines of many quickly resumed. To meet increased demand, New York Waterway added seven new routes. The company chartered vessels from up and down the Northeast coast, including whale-watching boats from Massachusetts, in order to run as many as 35 ferries during rush hour. Still the ferry system was stretched to capacity, and Port Authority officials announced that they were racing to build a new ferry terminal near Battery Park to cut New Jersey commute times in half.

On an average weekday before September 11, 2001, 32,000 passengers had ridden New York Waterway ferries. By December, that number jumped to nearly 60,000. "If September 11 had not happened, we would have reached this level of ridership in five to six years, but we reached it almost overnight," company president Arthur Imperatore Jr. told *The New York Times* at the close of 2001. "It has raised the awareness of a lot of new people about the capability of ferries. They're not a toy. They're serious transportation." To a large extent, he argued, the ferries helped hold Lower Manhattan together for months following the attacks.

The Staten Island Ferry had also done its part to normalize commuting routines when service resumed on September 17, despite new regulations prohibiting vehicles aboard the boats. By late December, the New York City DOT reported that total ridership aboard both public and private ferries had more than doubled since the attacks. By April 2002, ferry use grew 91 percent, reaching the highest levels since the 1940s. All told, nearly a dozen new ferry routes had been established, and over the course of six weeks, an existing Battery Park terminal was reopened, and a railroad barge was retrofitted to create a new six-slip ferry landing at Pier A.

Amico was upgrading the New Jersey side as well. On the second weekend following the attacks, he was working to revamp a small pier float at Colgate, just north of Paulus Hook and directly across the Hudson from North Cove, which previously could only serve a single boat. To accommodate the variety of different watercraft now arriving on the scene, each with different docking configurations, he had to adapt the pier with both bow- and side-loading capabilities. The job involved driving pilings, and he took his usual approach, checking to see if the pilings that he was installing were vertical by lining them up with a tall building. "I turned around to see if the pilings were straight by looking at the World Trade Center, like I would usually do," he recalled in an interview some months later. "Of course, the towers were gone. And I burst out in tears."

—⚬⚬⚬—

As new infrastructure was built to accommodate the "new normal," the crucial work of defending the harbor continued. Taking on that responsibility were Coast Guard personnel like Boatswain's Mate Carlos Perez, regularly assigned to New York harbor, as well as Coast Guard members (reserve and otherwise) who'd been called in to serve the region. With the establishment of an incident command center at Fort Wadsworth, 1,500 active duty, reserve, and auxiliary personnel from Coast Guard stations

Captain James Parese has retired. On September 11, 2016, another captain stands at the east-facing helm, wearing dark shades and a white-collared shirt with black- and gold-striped epaulets. He peers out through the glass with a closed-lipped expression while below him, hundreds, possibly thousands of passengers board the double-ended ferryboat. If you ask the crewman on deck for the captain's name he'll tell you Henry, but nothing more. "It's our policy not to give out that information," he'll explain.

The Staten Island Ferry eases out of Whitehall Terminal's Slip One, and Manhattan recedes into the distance. Clusters of buildings, old and new, reveal the island's ever-changing cityscape. In the foreground, the curved, mirror-sheathed facade of a 1988, wedge-shaped building at 17 State Street reflects white clouds in blue sky. For a brief moment, the green pyramidal crown of the former Bank of Manhattan Building, which in 1930 spent less than a month as the world's tallest, peeks out above 17 State before disappearing once again as the ferryboat pulls farther into the harbor. A blinking white light atop the spire of the nation's new tallest building, 1 World Trade Center, flashes in the blue sky.

Soon the whole mixed-use harbor comes into view. Against a backdrop of blue, white, and orange-and-white striped shipping cranes that hover above stacks of multicolored containers, vessels of all sorts dart about the Upper Bay past others biding their time at anchor. Recreational sailboats and charter yachts pass rows of cargo barges piled high with stone. Water taxis and fast ferries shuttle passengers to and fro just off Liberty Island where, above her muddied gray and green gown, Lady Liberty's polished torch gleams bright in the sun. Statue of Liberty ferryboats make their runs bringing her visitors, and today each ferry is accompanied by two orange-hulled, defender-class Coast Guard response boats, well armed.

It wasn't always this way. Less than a year after the 2001 attacks, the head of the Coast Guard's Strategic Analysis Office, Captain Robert Ross, told *National Defense* magazine that the task of building up Coast Guard security operations was as overwhelming as eating an elephant. "We are trying to carve this elephant up in slices that we can swallow without choking," he said. "We got here through many, many years of neglecting the threats that a lot of people knew were there. . . . We are not going to fix these problems overnight." He went on to acknowledge that the waterways will always present vulnerabilities, and that "we cannot prevent everything."

A decade and a half later, the new captain of the port, Captain Michael Day—who, after a stint as deputy sector commander in San Francisco, assumed command of Sector New York in July 2015—said that the current culture of vigilance combined with an even stronger "unity of purpose and effort" than that which he extolled in 2001 have created a far safer port. Today's security systems are much more integrated across agencies than they were before, Day said, mentioning the daily intelligence briefings that he receives from the NYPD as one example. "There's better shared awareness of what's going on," he explained, adding that the "shared consciousness" that grew out of overcoming the World Trade Center attacks together is rooted in a "common frame of reference," a recognition of the devastation that occurred in this city.

These important, although somewhat intangible, differences between then and now have also been reinforced by the very tangible reality of infrastructure. The Port of New York and New Jersey has received what Day called the "enabling mechanism of fairly robust port security grants." Not only does the Coast Guard have better tools and equipment, it also has better systems in place for addressing security issues with a multiagency approach. And now, for the first time, there is an actual maritime evacuation plan.

A key participant in the development of that plan was the Port Authority's Bethann Rooney who spent years building the port's security infrastructure from the ground up. The port has been completely transformed since the open-docks, "lawn chair" days. Immediately after September 11, the Harbor Ops Committee established a security subcommittee, which Rooney cochaired with the Coast Guard. "Discussions began in earnest about the whole gamut of security and emergency response," Rooney explained.

"We said there were five tenets of security: awareness, prevention, protection, response, and
recovery. In the response arena we started looking at, well, what if we had to do this maritime
response again and needed to evacuate Manhattan? Informal discussions started to look at after-
action reports and critiques of what worked and
what didn't work, what could we do better, and
how do we formalize that?"

In the midst of those discussions, on a Thursday in August
2003, just after 4 P.M., the largest blackout in U.S. history shut
down New York City, along with the whole Northeast. This
was not a "calling all boats" situation, Rooney was quick to
explain. "The immediacy and urgency to get out of the city
wasn't there" in the same way it had been in 2001. Instead,
transportation shutdowns caused by the power outages that left
commuters stranded in Manhattan stretched the ferry system
beyond capacity. The blackout experience led to the formation
of a Harbor Ops Maritime Evacuation Subcommittee, which
then developed and exercised a plan explicitly for maritime
evacuation. The work group collected extensive data about all
the various ferry landings and docking options, numbers and
capacities of different vessels, as well as their needs and features including carriage limitations and docking requirements,
among other considerations. Since then, key port players,
including the NYPD, New York City OEM, Coast Guard, Port
Authority, public and private ferryboat operators, and others,
have participated in the development of, and exercised, the plan
that everyone hopes will never be used.

On an ongoing basis, members of the port community continue to periodically gather in a room to address what-if scenarios, responding to a specific situation by marshaling resources
represented on paper, white boards, and nautical charts, using
magnets, markers, and Post-it notes. "You do it as if it was the
real time, the real day," said Rooney.

> "So, New York Waterway, it's a Thursday evening,
> January 26 at 5:53. Massive event in New York City.
> What do you have to respond? What do you have
> ready now? Start deploying it. How many assets do
> you have tied up because you don't have captains?
> How long will it take you to get those captains and
> crews there so you can get under way?"

Beyond the maritime evacuation, Rooney explained, port officials exercise all types of scenarios all over the port. Every one of the 180-plus facilities that move people and goods across the dock is required to conduct an exercise each year that tests multiple parts of the facility's specific plan. These drills are mandated by legislation that Rooney worked with Congress to help craft. "We had to go from nothing to complying with a set of international and domestic regulations and trying to figure out, what are the threats that we need to protect ourselves from?"

Still, one key lesson from the September 11 boat lift remains top of mind for people like Captain Day: the success of the evacuation evolved in large part out of its spontaneous, unplanned nature. "What's that old saying?" asked Day. "No plan survives first contact with the enemy."

In keeping with the example set by the former captain of the port Admiral Bennis, Day's leadership approach emphasizes trusting his teams to take in the information available in the moment and use their best judgment about what positive actions will make things better. "I certainly wouldn't want to second-guess what they're doing on scene. That's part of our DNA, part of our [Coast Guard] culture, to push on-scene initiative," he explained. When it comes to planning, as Day sees it, it's crucial that the blueprint for managing any security situation must be focused on presenting *options* rather than *prescriptions*. A critical part of any plan has to include the reality that "we're going to adapt and improvise for the best outcome possible."

That said, systemic improvements to protocols and equipment are still an essential component of increased port security. Since September 11, the Port Authority has invested $38 million in security programs, technology, and infrastructure, as well as instituting all sorts of new policies and procedures. In recognition of the effectiveness of the agency's efforts, in June 2014 the Coast Guard awarded the Port Authority the Rear Admiral Richard E. Bennis Award, which honors an exceptional commitment to the security of the United States and the marine transportation system. "The Port Authority of New York and New Jersey's security program ensures that we can provide a safe and secure environment for our customers and employees while having a robust, dynamic security program at our port facilities," Richard Larrabee said at the time. "Receiving this award is especially meaningful given that we are the first recipients and the award is named after Admiral Richard Bennis, who on 9/11 was the Coast Guard captain of the port here in New York."

The award was established to honor Bennis following his death in August of 2003 from incurable melanoma that had spread to his lungs and his brain. Bennis had already been struggling with cancer when he was called upon to lead the Coast Guard's response in the aftermath of the deadliest terrorist attack on U.S. soil. (In fact, on September 10, 2001, doctors had removed the staples that had sutured the rear admiral's head after brain surgery.) But by March 2002, Bennis's health had seemed to improve, and he had taken a post as chief of the Maritime and Land Security Office within a new agency, the Transportation Security Administration, which would soon become part of the newly established Department of Homeland Security. When he accepted the position to develop strategies to protect the nation's rails, roads, pipelines, and waterways from attacks, he took half a dozen Coast Guard officials with him, including Captain Patrick Harris. Harris served as the Maritime and Land Security Office's first chief of staff until retiring in 2003.

Also lost in the years since 2001 were John Krevey, who offered up his public-access Pier 63 as a dock for dinner boats ferrying passengers, and John Doswell, the maritime event producer who helped him manage the crowds.

Fifteen years after the events that defined so many maritime careers and permanently altered so many lives, Staten Island Ferry riders crowd against the railings to see the New York harbor sights unfold.

They watch as the huge, 310-foot-long ferryboat swings wider than usual, a bit farther out to sea, to make sure to avoid crossing the bow of a Hapag-Lloyd container ship. As the ferry approaches the ship, the massive passenger vessel seems tiny, making it clear just how gargantuan the cargo vessel is. Doubtless, in accordance with maritime law, a Sandy Hook Pilot stationed in the bridge is guiding the ship through the harbor. He or she met the ship before it passed beneath the Verrazano–Narrows Bridge, arriving in a launch that lined up with the vessel, like a fly on an elephant, to position the pilot for a climb up the rope ladder slung over the ship's side.

Designed for secure ocean crossings, the *Houston Express*, from Hamburg, lacks the maneuverability to make sharp turns in a crowded port. So at least two tugs are needed to assist the ship's passage, gently nudging the 1,000-plus-foot-long vessel in a coordinated dance choreographed according to the pilot's commands. Markings labeled "TUG" indicate the spots on the hull where this nudging should occur.

As the ferry takes the ship's stern, the first tugboat comes into view, bringing up the rear. Two newer tugs are already in position on the vessel's port side. They'll provide the thrust necessary to keep the containership on course as it hooks to the west, bound for a New Jersey container port.

On the opposite side of the ferry, before the great sweeping arcs formed by the suspension cables of the double-decked Verrazano–Narrows Bridge, a cluster of barges and a modern articulated tug barge unit (in which the tug is coupled directly to the barge with a hinged connection at the boat's bow) wait at anchor for freed-up dock space or a fair tide.

As the ferry advances toward Staten Island, the expanse of blue-black water to the east is bookended by two clusters of skyscrapers. Manhattan's historic financial district rises on the right while across the Hudson at Paulus Hook, just north of the

Colgate Clock, stands "Wall Street West," so called for its concentration of financial company offices. Jersey City marks the southern boundary of the "Gold Coast of New Jersey," a string of rapidly expanding riverfront towns where a patchwork of developments once struggling with high vacancy rates and canceled projects has sprouted into a grove of high rises. The current land grab that has buyers snatching up property at record-high prices was exactly the real estate boom that Arthur Imperatore Sr. was banking on when he founded New York Waterway in Weehawken.

As the Staten Island Ferry captain lines up the ferry for the final approach into the slip, a crew member's voice, low and thick with a New York accent, rings out over the loudspeaker. He informs passengers, multiple times, that they cannot remain aboard this ferry in hopes of a round trip. "Upon arrival all passengers must leave this boat. This boat will be going out of service and will not be returning back to Manhattan. If you wish to return to Manhattan, exit through the terminal and wait for the next available boat."

The next available boat, *Spirit of America*, is waiting in the adjacent slip. In honor of today's anniversary, the flag mounted on its upper deck flies at half-mast. Some ferry passengers will surely take notice. Although they are unlikely to have heard about the role that New York harbor's vessels and crews played in delivering people to safety in the aftermath of the World Trade Center attacks, most tourists and natives alike recognize the significance of this day. Who could forget where they were, whom they were with, and what they were doing on September 11, 2001? It's a date burned into the memories of a generation. But, 15 years later, as is proper, we remember, we memorialize, we pay respects, and then we—including the mariners of New York harbor—get back to work.

# Epilogue

Fifteen years later, I, too, have learned how to get back to work, making peace with the haunting memories churned up by each anniversary. Today I can more readily perceive the helpers through the horrors. And the helpers. . . The helpers are what still reverberates a decade and a half later. They have reconstructed my faith in the human soul.

When I returned home to Brooklyn from Ground Zero on September 14, 2001, the earth seemed to have shifted on its axis. My life felt irrevocably altered, but I found it difficult to understand or express exactly what had changed.

The boat on which I served as assistant engineer, retired fireboat *John J. Harvey*, was lauded as a "hero of the harbor," and so, by extension, was the boat's crew. But the classic September 11 hero narrative never sat well with me. It seemed rooted in some arbitrary separation between those who help and those who don't. It seemed to hinge on some diminishment of our collective human potential.

Many people who showed up to work at Ground Zero—firefighters, ironworkers, engineers, journalists, chiropractors, medics, people from trades of all kinds—did so out of a sense of duty and professional honor. Yet, even those with no obviously applicable expertise possessed skills that could be useful, so they used them. These acts have always struck me as less about heroism and more about pragmatism, resourcefulness, and simple human decency. If you have the wherewithal, you step up.

In her book *A Paradise Built in Hell*, Rebecca Solnit crystallizes perfectly the "resilient, resourceful, generous, empathic, and brave" nature of humans confronting disasters:

> "When all the ordinary divides and patterns are shattered, people step up—not all, but the great preponderance—to become their brothers' keepers. And that purposefulness and connectedness bring joy even amid death, chaos, fear, and loss. Were we to know and believe this, our sense of what is possible at any time might change. . . . Horrible in itself, disaster is sometimes a door back into paradise, the paradise at least in which we are who we hope to be, do the work we desire, and are each our sister's and brother's keeper."

Stepping up, with purpose, even in the absence of a plan, allows us to foster the connectedness that is the very manifestation of humanity.

# Acknowledgments

THIS BOOK IS based on the first-person accounts of people who shared with me their proudest and their darkest moments, some recounting for the first time their experiences during those fraught hours. I am humbled by their generosity and awed by the resourcefulness, joint action, compassion, and power of New York harbor's maritime community, harnessed that day to save countless souls.

Innumerable people helped me locate interview sources, including: Bonnie Aldinger, Brandon Brewer, Andy Brooks, Jim Campanelli, Rose Craig, Dan Croce, John Doswell, Jim Ellis, Leslie Gilbert Elman, Linda Galloway Farrell, Tom Ferrie, Nancy Gamerman, Della Louise Hasselle, Pete Johansen, Patrick Kinnier, Edward Knoblauch, Kaitlin Knoblick, Eric Kosper, Erika Kuciw, Madison Meadows, Harry Milkman, Ellen Neuborne, Rose Newnham, Timothy O'Brien, Kelley O'Connor-Iacobaccio, Kelly Palazzi, Jeanne Park, Jean Preece, Carolina Salguero, Jenna Schnuer, Skipper Shaffer, Sue Shapiro, Rich Siller, Christian Sorensen, Charlie Suisman, Christina Sun, Russell Tippets, Alex Weisler, Lewis Werner, Stephanie Wien, and Fred Woolverton.

Huge thank-yous to Paul Amico, Pete Capelotti, Huntley Gill, Pat Harris, Chris Havern, Tim Ivory, James Kendra, Bob Lenney, Greg Scharfstein, and Tricia Wachtendorf for answering research questions of all sorts. Generous assistance also came from Staceyann Chin and Myrna Shinbaum. Instrumental to my reporting were photographs taken/provided by Robert Deutsch, Greg Frietas, Jerry Grandinetti, Greg Hanchrow, Pete Johansen, Angela Krevey, Karen Lacey, Mike Littlefield, Carolina Salguero, Mort Starobin, Rick Thornton, and Fred Wehner, as well as the officers of the NYPD Aviation Unit.

I'm grateful to Molly Mulhern for dreaming up this project and trusting me to write it, Janet Robbins for patience while I tied up loose ends, and Christopher Brown for shepherding the hardcover to the finish line and then permitting its rebirth in paperback.

I'm deeply indebted to Michael McGandy and the whole Three Hills/Cornell University Press team—Martyn Beeny, Adriana Ferriera, Clare Jones, Mike Morris, Ange Romeo-Hall, and Brock Schnoke—for recognizing the importance of this history, bringing this paperback to life, and helping the boat lift story reach new readers.

Thank you to the brilliant cartographer Mike Bechthold for taking such care while making new maps for this edition. I am truly honored that

Mitchell Zuckoff, author of the extraordinary *Fall and Rise*, agreed to share his unique vantage point, putting into larger context the role of the maritime evacuation on this landmark day.

I'm grateful to Spike Lee and his team, including Judy Aley and Cara Fitts, for documenting and spotlighting the stories of people who, in times of trouble, stand up to help others.

Thanks to Kent Barwick, Huntley Gill, Clay Hiles, Mark Kramer, Leslie Meredith, Ellen Neuborne, and Nancy Rawlinson for tremendous grant application help. Crucial financial support came from the Furthermore grants in publishing, a program of the J.M. Kaplan Fund, through the gracious sponsorship of the North River Historic Ship Society. Thanks also to James Gregorio for always being in my corner.

I cannot overstate the critical importance of the narrative counsel and cheerleading provided at pivotal moments by Trevor Corson, Burke Gerstenschlager, Katia Hetter, Mai Lauren Hoang, Anu Partanen, and Ellen Rubin. With their generous feedback and support, both Mark Kramer and Geoff Shandler granted me new ideas and narrative directions at make-or-break moments. Mark's steadfast guidance and mentorship has meant the world to me. Ben Rubin graciously read and commented on portions of this material far more times than anyone should ever have had to. And Nancy Rawlinson rescued the book when it was headed for the rocks. Without her warm-yet-tough coaching and keen editorial eye this book would not exist.

My life was forever changed the day I met my agent Joy Tutela, whose unflagging commitment, wise counsel, and friendship I treasure. There is no fiercer champion; I am so grateful to her and the David Black Agency team.

Thank you to the crew of fireboat *John J. Harvey* (especially the engineering team of John Browne, Jeff Griswold, Jim Travis, Paul Toledano, and Wendy Range) for keeping things running smoothly during my book-related absences. And thank you to all the loving and diligent sitters and teachers who gave me the peace of mind that permitted uninterrupted hours of writing.

Finally, the support and encouragement of my family, including Gretchen and Peter DuLong and Ellen and Harold Rubin, have made all things possible. A special thank you to my mother and sister, Molly Hanrahan, for heroic hotel-room baby wrangling that granted me the space to study craft each year at the ever-nourishing Power of Narrative conferences.

Thank you, Zillin and Jude, for your laughter, which lights the way. And thank you, Ben, for your love, patience, and unyielding support; for covering for me in countless ways; and for your unwavering belief in this project even when I was plagued with doubt. There are no words sufficient to express my gratitude for the chance to walk shoulder to shoulder with you on this journey.

# Vessel Participants in the Evacuation

While not comprehensive, this list, compiled by the late Captain John Doswell, includes many of the vessels that participated in the maritime evacuation of Manhattan on September 11, 2001.

*ABC-1*, Reynolds Shipyard, tug

*Abraham Lincoln*, New York Waterway, ferry

*Adak*, United States Coast Guard, island cutter-class patrol boat

*Adriatic Sea*, K-Sea Transportation Corp., tug

*Alexander Hamilton*, New York Waterway, ferry

*Amberjack V*, Amberjack V, fishing boat

*American Legion*, New York City Department of Transportation, ferry

*Anne*, Reid Stowe, schooner

*Bainbridge Island*, United States Coast Guard, island cutter-class patrol boat

*Barbara Miller*, Miller's Launch, tug

*Barker Boys*, Barker Marine Ltd., tug

*Baleen*, Pegasus Restoration Project, historic whaleboat

*Bergen Point*, Ken's Marine, tug

*Bernadette*, Hudson River Park Trust, workboat

*Blue Thunder*, United States Merchant Marine Academy, fishing boat

*Bravest*, New York Fast Ferry, ferry

*Brendan Turecamo*, Moran Towing Corp., tug

*Bruce A. McAllister*, McAllister Towing and Transportation Co. Inc., tug

*Capt. John*, John Connell, unknown

*Captain Dann*, Dann Ocean Towing, Inc., tug

*Catherine Turecamo*, Moran Towing Corp., tug

*Chelsea Screamer*, Kennedy Engine Company, Inc., tour boat

*Chesapeake*, unknown, unknown

*Christopher Columbus*, New York Waterway, ferry

*Circle Line VIII*, Circle Line/World Yacht, tour boat

*Circle Line XI*, Circle Line/World Yacht, tour boat

*Circle Line XII*, Circle Line/World Yacht, tour boat

*Circle Line XV*, Circle Line/World Yacht, tour boat

*Circle Line XVI*, Circle Line/World Yacht, tour boat

*Coral Sea*, K-Sea Transportation Corp., tug

*Diana Moran*, Moran Towing Corp., tug

*Dottie J*, United States Merchant Marine Academy, fishing boat

*Driftmaster*, United States Army Corps of Engineers, drift collection vessel

*Eileen McAllister*, McAllister Towing and Transportation Co. Inc., tug

*Elizabeth Weeks*, Weeks Marine Inc., tug

*Emily Miller*, Miller's Launch, tug

*Empire State*, New York Waterway, ferry

*Excalibur*, VIP Yacht Cruises, dinner/cruise boat

*Express Explorer*, Express Marine, Inc., tug

*Finest*, New York Fast Ferry, ferry

*Fiorello La Guardia*, New York Waterway, ferry

*Frank Sinatra*, New York Waterway, ferry

*Franklin Reinauer*, Reinauer Transportation Companies, tug

*Garden State*, New York Waterway, ferry

*Gelberman*, United States Army Corps of Engineers, drift collection vessel

*George Washington*, New York Waterway, ferry

*Giovanni Da Verrazano*, New York Waterway, ferry

*Gov. Herbert H. Lehman*, New York City Department of Transportation, ferry

*Growler*, United States Merchant Marine Academy, tug

*Gulf Guardian*, Skaugen PetroTrans Inc., tug

*Hatton*, United States Army Corps of Engineers, work vessel

*Hawser*, United States Coast Guard, small harbor tug

*Hayward*, United States Army Corps of Engineers, drift collection vessel

*Henry Hudson*, New York Waterway, ferry

*Horizon*, VIP Yacht Cruises, dinner/cruise boat

*Hurricane I*, United States Merchant Marine Academy, utility boat

*Hurricane II*, United States Merchant Marine Academy, utility boat

*JC*, unknown, unknown

*Jersey City Police Emergency Service Unit boat*, Jersey City Police Emergency Service, police boat

*John D. McKean*, Fire Department City Of New York, fireboat

*John F. Kennedy*, New York City Department of Transportation, ferry

*John J. Harvey*, John J. Harvey, Ltd., retired Fire Department City Of New York fireboat

*John Jay*, New York Waterway, ferry

*John Reinauer*, Reinauer Transportation Companies, tug

*Katherine Walker*, United States Coast Guard, cutter

*Kathleen Turecamo*, Moran Towing Corp., tug

*Kathleen Weeks*, Weeks Marine Inc., tug

*Ken Johnson*, Interport Pilots Agency, pilot boat

*Kevin C. Kane*, Fire Department City Of New York, Fireboat

*Kimberley Turecamo*, Moran Towing Corp., tug

*Kings Pointer*, United States Merchant Marine Academy, training vessel

*Kristy Ann Reinauer*, Reinauer Transportation Companies, tug

*Lady*, Lady Cruise Lines, dinner/cruise boat

*Launch No. 5*, USCG Auxiliary, retired police launch

*Lexington*, VIP Yacht Cruises, dinner/cruise boat

*Line*, United States Coast Guard, small harbor tug

*Little Lady*, Liberty State Park Water Taxi, ferry

*Margaret Moran*, Moran Towing Corp., tug

*Marie J. Turecamo*, Moran Towing Corp., tug

*Mary Alice*, DonJon Marine Co. Inc., tug

*Mary Gellately*, Gellately Petroleum and Towing Corp., tug

*Mary L. McAllister*, McAllister Towing and Transportation Co. Inc., tug

*Maryland*, K-Sea Transportation Corp, tug

*Maverick*, United States Merchant Marine Academy, pilot launch

*McAllister Sisters*, McAllister Towing and Transportation Co. Inc., tug

*Millennium*, Fox Navigation, ferry

*Miller Girls*, Miller's Launch, tug

*Miriam Moran*, Moran Towing Corp., tug

*Miss Circle Line*, Circle Line-Statue of Liberty Ferry, Inc., tour boat

*Miss Ellis Island*, Circle Line-Statue of Liberty Ferry, Inc., tour boat

*Morgan Reinauer*, Reinauer Transportation Companies, tug

*Nancy Moran*, Moran Towing Corp., tug

*New Jersey*, New York Waterway, ferry

*Ocean Explorer*, unknown, unknown

*Odin*, K-Sea Transportation Corp., tug

*Paul Andrew*, DonJon Marine Co. Inc., tug

*Penn II*, Penn Maritime Inc., tug

*Penobscot Bay*, United States Coast Guard, bay-class icebreaking tug

*Peter Gellately*, Gellately Petroleum and Towing Corp., tug

*New York*, Sandy Hook Pilots Association, pilot boat

*Port Service*, Leevac Marine, tug

*Poseidon*, United States Merchant Marine Academy, patrol boat

*Potomac*, unknown, unknown

*Powhatan*, DonJon Marine Co. Inc., tug

*Queen of Hearts*, Promoceans /Affairs Afloat, dinner/cruise boat

*Resolute*, McAllister Towing and Transportation Co. Inc., tug

*Ridley*, United States Coast Guard, cutter

*Robert Fulton*, New York Waterway, ferry

*Robert Livingston*, New York Waterway, ferry

*Romantica*, VIP Yacht Cruises, dinner/cruise boat

*Royal Princess*, VIP Yacht Cruises, dinner/cruise boat

*Safety III*, United States Merchant Marine Academy, utility boat

*Safety IV*, United States Merchant Marine Academy, utility boat

*Samantha Miller*, Miller's Launch, tug

*Sandy G*, Warren George, Inc., unknown

*Sassacus*, Fox Navigation, ferry

*Sea Service*, Leevac Marine, tug

*Seastreak Brooklyn*, SeaStreak America, Inc., ferry

*Seastreak Liberty*, SeaStreak America, Inc., ferry

*SeaStreak Manhattan*, SeaStreak America, Inc., ferry

*Seastreak New York*, SeaStreak America, Inc., ferry

*Smoke II*, Fire Department City Of New York, fireboat

*Spartan Service*, Leevac Marine, tug

*Spirit of New Jersey*, Spirit Cruises, dinner/cruise boat

*Spirit of New York*, Spirit Cruises, dinner/cruise boat

*Spirit of the Hudson*, Spirit Cruises, dinner/cruise boat

*Stapleton Service*, Leevac Marine, tug

*Star of Palm Beach*, Promoceans /Affairs Afloat, dinner/cruise boat

*Sterling*, Lady Liberty Cruises, dinner/cruise boat

*Storm*, United States Merchant Marine Academy, search and rescue vessel

*Sturgeon Bay*, United States Coast Guard, bay-class icebreaking tug

*Susan Miller*, Miller's Launch, tug

*Tahoma*, United States Coast Guard, cutter

*Tatobam*, Fox Navigation, ferry.

*Taurus*, K-Sea Transportation Corp., tug

Tender for tugboat *Bertha*, Darren Vigilant, motorboat

*Theodore Roosevelt*, New York Waterway, ferry

*Turecamo Boys*, Moran Towing Corp., tug

*Turecamo Girls*, Moran Towing Corp., tug

*Twin Tube*, Reynolds Shipyard Corp., tug

*Unk*, United States Coast Guard, motor lifeboat

Various New York State Department of Environmental Conservation work boats

Various fishing boats

Various Nassau County police/patrol boats

Various New Jersey state and local police/patrol boats

Various NYPD police/patrol boats

Various other vessels

Various Staten Island Ferries

Various United States Coast Guard utility boats

Various United States Coast Guard rigid hull inflatables

*Virginia Weeks*, Weeks Marine Inc., tug

*Vivian Roehrig*, C & R Harbor Towing, tug

*West New York*, New York Waterway, ferry

*Wings of the Morning*, United States Merchant Marine Academy, utility boat

*Wire*, United States Coast Guard, small harbor tug

*Yogi Berra*, New York Waterway, ferry

# NOTES

**PART ONE: The Situation**

*Chapter One: "It was a jet. It was a jet. It was a jet."*

4     *2,977 people:* Associated Press, "List of 2,977 Sept. 11 Victims," *Daily Herald,* 2/6/17, http://www.dailyherald.com/article/20110909/news/110909868/.

       The 2,977 total includes 2,753 killed at the World Trade Center (as well as three victims who later died of respiratory disease resulting from dust exposure and whose deaths were reclassified as homicides by the New York City Medical Examiner's Office), 184 killed at the Pentagon, and 40 killed on United Airlines Flight 93 in Pennsylvania. It does not include the 19 hijackers.

7     *400,000 to 500,000 civilians:* It is virtually impossible to ascertain exactly how many people were transported off Manhattan by boat. The earliest estimates released by the Coast Guard topped out at 1 million. Later estimates, such as those published in 2003, ranged between 350,000 and 500,000. (Dan Croce, "Attack on New York: The First Response," *Coast Guard Journal of Safety at Sea, Proceedings of the Marine Safety Council,* April–June 2003, 7.)

       A 2002 U.S. Department of Transportation report cited Port Authority estimates that New York Waterway ferries evacuated 160,000 people and 200,000 to 300,000 people were transported aboard other vessels (U.S. Department of Transportation's John A. Volpe National Transportation Systems Center, "Effects of Catastrophic Events on Transportation System Management and Operations: New York City—September 11," 15, 2/6/17, https://ntl.bts.gov/lib/jpodocs/repts_te/14129.htm).

       Perhaps the most precise figures have been compiled by University of Delaware disaster researchers James Kendra and Tricia Wachtendorf, who combined Manhattan daytime population estimates from a 2012 NYU Wagner School report (Mitchell L. Moss and Carson Qing, Rudin Center for Transportation Policy and Management Wagner School of Public Service, New York University, "The Dynamic Population of Manhattan," March 2012) with an analysis of WTC evacuees completed by researchers Rae Zimmerman and Martin F. Sherman (Rae Zimmerman and Martin F. Sherman, "To Leave an Area After Disaster: How Evacuees from the WTC Buildings Left the WTC Area Following the Attacks," *Risk Analysis,* Vol. 31, No. 5, 2011) to conclude that approximately 415,000 people traveled by boat that morning.

8–9    *quick tour of the numbers:* These port statistics represent 1999 figures provided in a report produced annually by the Port Authority of New York and New Jersey. Port Authority representatives explained that its 2000 report was lost in the World Trade Center collapse and that no 2001 report was produced, given the agency's focus on recovery efforts in the aftermath of the attacks. A spokesperson confirmed that the 1999 figures provide an accurate picture of 2001 activity since the percent change between 1999 and 2001 tallies would have been negligible. Source: Michael Day, "Harbor Safety Committees: A Construct for Comprehensive Harbor Stewardship," (*2001*) 2001 International Oil Spill Conference Volume 2. *International Oil Spill Conference Proceedings: March 2001,* Vol. 2001, No. 2, 35-40, 8/17/16, http://ioscproceedings.org/doi/pdf/10.7901/2169-3358-2001-1-35.

11    *prevent vessel collisions:* "Vessel Traffic Services," United States Coast Guard Navigation Center, 2/6/17, http://www.navcen.uscg gov/?pageName=vtsMain.

12      *fitting centerpiece:* Brittany Fowler, "Then and Now: How New York
        City's World Trade Center has changed in the 14 years since the 9/11 ter-
        rorist attack," *Business Insider,* 2/6/17, http://www.businessinsider.com/
        world-trade-center-pictures-before-during-and-after-911-2015-9/#today-
        cond-nast-and-others-call-the-freedom-tower-home-but-we-will-never-
        forget-the-twin-structures-that-stood-there-before-17.
13      *50,000 people:* "Effects of Catastrophic Events," 6.
16      *less than a mile away:* Jim Dwyer and Kevin Flynn, *102 Minutes: The Unfor-
        gettable Story of the Fight to Survive Inside the Twin Towers,* New York: Times
        Books, 2005, 48.
16      *8:48:09:* "Manhattan dispatcher audio tape transcript," *The New York Times,*
        2/6/17, http://www.nytimes.com/packages/pdf/nyregion/wtctape1.1.pdf.
17      *Hayden later explained:* Peter Hayden testimony, May 18, 2004, videotaped.
        From National Commission on Terrorist Attacks, *The 9/11 Commission
        Report,* New York: W.W. Norton & Company, 2004, 291–2.
17      *each single trade center floor:* Dwyer and Flynn, *102 Minutes,* 50.
17      *strictly a rescue:* Peter Hayden testimony.
17      *to reach the upper floors:* Dwyer and Flynn, *102 Minutes,* 51.
18      *without elevators: Ibid.*
18      *"war footing": Ibid.,* 56.
18      *Level 4 marshaled: The 9/11 Commission Report,* 291.
18      *largest rescue operation: Ibid.,* 293.
19      *flight controllers had learned: Ibid.,* 20.
19      *FAA: Ibid.*
19      *NEADS ordered: Ibid.*
20      *16,400 to 18,800 people: Ibid.,* 316.
20      *daytime population:* Office of the New York State Comptroller, "The Trans-
        formation of Lower Manhattan's Economy," Report 4-2017, September 2016,
        1/26/17, 2, http://www.osc.state.ny.us/osdc/reports/rpt4-2017.pdf.
20      *island of Manhattan:* "Effects of Catastrophic Events," 3.
20      *weekdays in 2001: Ibid.,* 4.
21      *within minutes:* Dwyer and Flynn, *102 Minutes,* 174.


        Chapter 2: "Shut it down. Shut it down. Shut it down!"

22      *Kenneth Summers's choice:* Kenneth Summers, Smithsonian story
        #6382, The September 11 Digital Archive, 17 December 2003, 6/7/16,
        http://911digitalarchive.org/smithsonian/details/6382.
23      *more than 60 stores:* "Effects of Catastrophic Events," 6.
27      *mass evacuations:* Dwyer and Flynn, *102 Minutes,* 129.
34      *grown up around:* Phillip Lopate, *Seaport: New York's Vanished Waterfront,*
        Washington: Smithsonian Books, 2004, 1.
35      *five container facilities:* Author interview with Bethann Rooney, assistant
        director for the Port Department, Port Authority of New York and New
        Jersey, 1/26/17.
38      *radio channels: The 9/11 Commission Report,* 301.
38      *transmissions unintelligible: Ibid.,* 283.
39      *chiefs in the lobby: Ibid.,* 299.
39      *Tactical 1: Ibid.,* 301.
40      *"ride heavy": Ibid.,* 297.


        Chapter 3: "NEW YORK CITY CLOSED TO ALL TRAFFIC"

42      *Port Authority's retort:* Dwyer and Flynn, *102 Minutes,* 58.
49      *fireproofing material: Ibid.,* 58 and 67.
49      *finished about 30: Ibid.,* 58.

50    *this heat:* "Debunking the 9/11 Myths: Special Report—The World Trade Center," *Popular Mechanics,* March 2005, 2/6/17, http://www.popularmechanics.com/military/a6384/debunking-911-myths-world-trade-center/.
50    *about 50 minutes:* Dwyer and Flynn, *102 Minutes,* 207.
50    *at 9:13:* The 9/11 Commission Report, 24.
51    *force of the collapse:* Dwyer and Flynn, *102 Minutes,* 20. Steven Ashley, "When the Twin Towers Fell," *Scientific American,* October 2001, 8/12/13, http://www.scientificamerican.com/article.cfm?id=when-the-twin-towers-fell.

**PART TWO: The Evacuation**

*Chapter 4: "I was gonna swim to Jersey."*

54    *professional honor:* James Kendra and Tricia Wachtendorf, *American Dunkirk,* Philadelphia: Temple University Press, 2016, 119.
56    *scientists have since calculated:* Dwyer and Flynn, *102 Minutes,* 212.
56    *500,000 ton mass:* Ashley, "When the Twin Towers Fell," http://www.scientificamerican.com/article.cfm?id= when-the-twin-towers-fell.
56    *enough power:* Dwyer and Flynn, *102 Minutes,* 212.
56–57 *actually breathing in:* Joanna Walters, "9/11 Health Crisis: Death Toll from Illness Nears Number Killed on Day of Attacks," *The Guardian,* September 11, 2016, 1/13/17, https://www.theguardian.com/us-news/2016/sep/11/9-11-illnesses-death-toll.
62    *police officer halted:* Dwyer and Flynn, *102 Minutes,* 172.
62    *Captain Paul Conlon:* FDNY Battalion Chief James McGrath, World Trade Center Task Force Interview with FDNY Captain Paul Conlon, File No 9110487, January 26, 2002, 2/6/17, http://graphics8.nytimes.com/packages/pdf/nyregion/20050812_WTC_GRAPHIC/9110487.PDF.
63    *rubbish bin aflame: Ibid.*
64    *top brass:* Dwyer and Flynn, *102 Minutes,* 204.
65    *"like little peanuts":* Mike Magee, *All Available Boats: The Evacuation of Manhattan Island on September 11, 2001,* New York: Spencer Books, 2002, 40.
70    *races around Manhattan:* Zach Schonbrunaug, "Swim Around Manhattan Is Saved From a Future as Murky as Its Waters," *The New York Times,* August 18, 2016, 2/6/17, http://www.nytimes.com/2016/08/19/sports/swim-around-manhattan-is-saved-from-a-future-as-murky-as-its-waters.html.

*Chapter 5: "It was like breathing dirt."*

72    *giant scissors:* Dwyer and Flynn, *102 Minutes,* 231.
72    *close to a thousand: Ibid.,* 229.
73    *22-inch-wide windows:* Evie T. Joselow, "World Trade Center, New York City," R. Stephen Sennott, Ed. *Encyclopedia of 20th-Century Architecture,* v. 3, New York: Fitzroy Dearborn, 2004, 1452.
74    *$90 million:* The 9/11 Commission Report, 280.
74    *enormous development project:* "History of the Twin Towers," The Port Authority of New York and New Jersey, 2/6/17, http://www.panynj.gov/wtcprogress/history-twin-towers.html.
75    *existing railway tunnels:* "PATH Rail History," The Port Authority of New York and New Jersey, 2/6/17, http://www.panynj.gov/about/history-path.html.
75    *in 1962: Ibid.*
77    *face of the towers:* Dwyer and Flynn, *102 Minutes,* 40.
77    *steel spandrel members:* Ashley, "When the Twin Towers Fell," http://www.scientificamerican.com/article.cfm?id= when-the-twin-towers-fell.
81    *85 percent:* The 9/11 Commission Report, 317.

Chapter 6: "We're in the water!"

86    *11 different companies:* Brian J. Cudahy, *Over and Back: The History of Ferryboats in New York Harbor,* New York: Fordham University Press, 1990, 340.
86    *city-run service: Ibid.,* 195.
87    *private ferries began: Ibid.,* 317.
90    *five-year training program:* Emily S. Rueb, "The Channel Masters of New York Harbor," *The New York Times,* November 17, 2016, 2/6/17, http://www.nytimes.com/2016/11/20/nyregion/at-sea-with-new-york-harbors-channel-masters.html.
91    *Sandy Hook Pilots:* Kendra and Wachtendorf, *American Dunkirk,* 107.
91–92  *OpSail plans: Ibid.,* 106

Chapter 7: "Gray ghosts"

98    *building had twisted:* Dwyer and Flynn, *102 Minutes,* 242.
100   *Kate Silverton:* Name has been changed in accordance with the minor child's mother's wishes.
101   *Susan Silverton:* Name has been changed in accordance with source's wishes.
103   *Military Ocean Terminal:* "Brooklyn Army Terminal History," BKLYN Army Terminal, 2/6/17, https://www.bklynarmyterminal.com/building-information/history/.
108   *New Jersey EMS official:* A.J. Heightman, "Exodus Across the Hudson," *Journal of Emergency Medical Services: Out of the Darkness,* September 2011, v. 2, 9/16/16, http://www.jems.com/content/dam/jems/PDFs/Vol%202_New%20Jersey.pdf, 5.
109   *"all frontal burns":* Heightman, "Exodus Across the Hudson," 11–12.

Chapter 8: "A sea of boats"

115   *I was sent there:* Kendra and Wachtendorf, *American Dunkirk,* 113.
118   *marshaling stations:* P.J. Capelotti, *Rogue Wave: The U.S. Coast Guard on and after 9/11,* Washington, D.C.: U.S. Coast Guard Historians Office, 2003, 21.
118   *team aboard the pilot boat:* Magee, *All Available Boats,* 58.
127   *Robert Fulton debuted:* George Matteson, *Tugboats of New York,* New York: New York University Press, 2005, 1.
127   *observers described:* Kirkpatrick Sale, *The Fire of His Genius: Robert Fulton and the American Dream,* New York: Simon and Schuster, 2002, 120.
128   *steam ferryboats:* Matteson, *Tugboats of New York,* 21.
128   *vessels doubled in size: Ibid.,* 23.
128   *limited call: Ibid.,* 25.
128–129 *diesel engine: Ibid.,* 224.
129   *critical industries: Ibid.,* 1.
129   *shift to containerization: Ibid.,* 214.
129   *by the early 2000s: Ibid.,* 220.
129   *"a sea of tugboats":* Magee, *All Available Boats,* 66.
133   *27 tugboats evacuated:* Norman Brouwer, "All Available Boats," *Seaport* magazine, Vol. XXXVII, Number 2 and 3, Spring/Summer 2002, 9.

Chapter 9: "I need a boat."

140   *row of grand buildings:* New York City WPA Writers' Project, *A Maritime History of New York,* second edition, New York: Going Coastal Inc., 2005, 193.

143    *prompting the company:* Richard O. Aichele, "A Shining Light in Our Darkest Hour," *Professional Mariner,* #61, Dec/Jan 2002, http://www.professional-mariner.com/March-2007/A-shining-light-in-our-darkest-hour/.
143    *photographs showed thousands:* Brouwer, "All Available Boats," 10.
147    *involved in a relief effort:* David Tarnow, "All Available Boats: Harbor Voices from 9/11," Interview with John Krevey, commissioned by the South Street Seaport Museum, 1/26/17, https://beta.prx.org/stories/2196.
151    *by nightfall:* "Effects of Catastrophic Events," Appendix, 19.
154    *best of our kind:* From written statement by Pat Harris.
158    *10,000 people:* John Erich, "Across the River from NYC, It Was 'John Wayne Time,'" *EMS World,* September 8, 2011, 2/6/17, http://www.emsworld.com/article/10364660/across-the-river-from-nyc-it-was-john-wayne-time.


**PART THREE: The Aftermath**

*Chapter 10: "We have to tell us what to do."*

162    *rules were broken:* Kendra and Wachtendorf, *American Dunkirk,* 125.
163    *eye for security: Ibid.,* 6.
169    *people left stranded:* "Effects of Catastrophic Events," 1.
171    *more than 50,000:* Brouwer, "All Available Boats," 10.
175    *distraught mother: Saved,* Episode 106, Animal Planet, August 2011 (video).


*Chapter 11: "Sell first, repent later."*

179    *trauma hospital:* "Chelsea Piers Plays Major Role in Days Following September 11th," *On The Piers,* Vol. 5, Issue 1, 1.
181    *frozen zone:* Steve Fishman, "Down By the Frozen Zone," *New York,* October 1, 2001, 2/6/17, http://nymag.com/nymetro/news/sept11/features/5201/.
186    *two opposing missions:* Croce, "Attack on New York," 7.
188    *nearly 60,000:* Lynda Richardson, "On the Busy Ferries, It's Steady as He Goes," *The New York Times,* December 19, 2001.
189    *April 2002:* "Effects of Catastrophic Events," 29.
189    *driving pilings:* Magee, *All Available Boats,* 54.
190    *cutters and small boats: Ibid.*


*Chapter 12: "Okay, I am in charge."*

191    *new rules:* Croce, "Attack on New York," 8.
193    *small but efficient operation:* Dan Barry, "Determined Volunteers Camped Out to Pitch In," *The New York Times,* September 23, 2001, 2/7/17, http://www.nytimes.com/2001/09/23/nyregion/a-nation-challenged-volunteers-determined-volunteers-camped-out-to-pitch-in.html.
196    *May 2002:* Michael E. Mazzei, *Pier 25: After the Fall,* 2/14/17, https://www.youtube.com/watch?v=-41APXH9YPQ&feature=youtu.be (video)
197    *small harbor:* Magee, *All Available Boats,* 22.
198    *by day's end:* McKinsey & Company, "Improving NYPD Emergency Preparedness and Response," August 19, 2002, 2/6/17, http://web.archive.org/web/20070615060709/http://www.nyc.gov/html/nypd/pdf/nypdemergency.pdf.


*Chapter 13: "They'd do it again tomorrow."*

199    *plume of toxins:* Centers for Disease Control and Prevention, "First Periodic Review of Scientific and Medical Evidence Related to Cancer for the World Trade Center Health Program," July 2011, 7.

199    *60,000 to 90,000 first responders:* Maoxin Wu, Ronald E. Gordon, Robin Herbert, Maria Padilla, Jacqueline Moline, David Mendelson, Virginia Litle, William D. Travis, and Joan Gil, "Case Report: Lung Disease in World Trade Center Responders Exposed to Dust and Smoke: Carbon Nanotubes Found in the Lungs of World Trade Center Patients and Dust Samples," *Environmental Health Perspectives,* 2010 Apr; 118(4): 1,1/20/17, https://www.ncbi.nlm.nih.gov/pmc/articles/PMC2854726/.

199    *too ill to work:* Department of Health and Human Services, Michael McPhillips testimony, James Zadroga 9/11 Health and Compensation Act of 2010, Public Meeting, March 3, 2011, 64, 2/6/17, https://www.cdc.gov/niosh/docket/archive/pdfs/NIOSH-226/0226-030311-MeetingTranscript.pdf.

201    *monitoring and treatment:* Centers for Disease Control, "WTC Health Program at a Glance, September 2016," 2/6/17, https://www.cdc.gov/wtc/ata-glance.html#overall.

201    *more than 75,000: Ibid.*

201    *at least 1,000 people:* Joanna Walters, "9/11 Health Crisis: Death Toll from Illness Nears Number Killed on Day of Attacks," *The Guardian,* September 11, 2016, 1/13/17, https://www.theguardian.com/us-news/2016/sep/11/9-11-illnesses-death-toll.

201    *chronic lung condition:* Anthony DePalma, "For the First Time New York Links a Death to 9/11 Dust," *The New York Times,* May 24, 2007, 2/6/17, http://www.nytimes.com/2007/05/24/nyregion/24dust.html.

201    *official death toll:* Associated Press, "List of 2,977 Sept. 11 Victims," *Daily Herald,* 2/6/17, http://www.dailyherald.com/article/20110909/news/110909868/.

202    *414 first responders:* Inae Oh and Nick Wing, "16 Sobering Numbers that Remind Us to Honor the Sacrifice of 9/11 Responders," *The Huffington Post,* September 11, 2004, 2/6/17, http://www.huffingtonpost.com/2014/09/11/911-first-responders_n_5797398.html.

204    *expand its maritime operations:* Al Baker, "Fire Dept. Revamps Approach to Emergencies on the City's Waterways, or Nearby," *The New York Times,* January 14, 2011, 2/6/17, http://www.nytimes.com/2011/01/15/nyregion/15fire.html?_r=1&pagewanted=print.

204    *same mission: Ibid.*

204    *one was dubbed:* FDNY Annual Report 2012/2013, 7, 2/6/17, http://www.nyc.gov/html/fdny/pdf/publications/annual_reports/2012_annual_report.pdf.

204    *their construction: Ibid.*

206    *estimated 25,000 children:* "9/11 Health: Children," The City of New York, 2/6/17, http://www.nyc.gov/html/doh/wtc/html/children/children.shtml.

206–207  *health of 985 children:* S.D. Stellman, P.A. Thomas, S. Osahan, et. al., "Respiratory Health of 985 Children Exposed to the World Trade Center Disaster: Report on World Trade Center Health Registry Wave 2 Follow-up, 2007–2008," *Journal of Asthma.* 2013 Feb 18, 2/6/17, http://www.ncbi.nlm.nih.gov/pubmed/23414223

*Chapter 14: September 11, 2016*

210    *sign on the wall:* "U.S. Coast Guard Maritime Security (MARSEC) Levels," U.S. Coast Guard, 2/7/17, https://www.uscg.mil/safetylevels/whatismarsec.asp.

211    *National Defense magazine:* Roxana Tiron, "Port Security Will Improve, But Gradually," *National Defense* magazine, July 2002, 2/6/17, http://www.nationaldefensemagazine.org/archive/2002/July/Pages/Port_Security4047.aspx?PF=1.

*Epilogue*

219    Rebecca Solnit, *A Paradise Built in Hell: The Extraordinary Communities that Arise in Disaster,* New York: Penguin Books, 2009, 3 and 8.

# Index

Academy Bus Company, 146
Aldinger, Bonnie, 22–24, 148–149
*American Dunkirk* (Kendra and
    Wachtendorf), 162
American Merchant Mariners' Memorial,
    209
Amico, Paul, 83–85, 134–136, 186–188, 189
Automatic Identification System (AIS), 210

*Baleen*, 155–157
Battery, 44, 51, 58, 60, 76, 80, 95, 114, 131–
    133, 137, 144, 150, 161, 180, 184, 197
Battery Park, 106, 118, 166, 188–189, 209
Battery Park City, 67, 70, 100, 122, 147,
    187, 194
Bennis, Richard E., 11–12, 31, 162–163,
    185, 186, 215
bodies, falling/jumping, 29, 37, 43, 62, 67,
    98, 101
Boeing 707 ad, 42
Borrone, Lillian, 197
Bouley, David, 193
Boulud, Daniel, 193
bridges
    closing of, vi, 46–47, 52, 116, 149
    effect of on commute, 75, 86–87
    reopening of, 191
Brooklyn Army Terminal, 103, 138
building upgrades, 74
Burns, Donald, 18

Campanelli, Jim, 37, 58, 110, 122, 124,
    125–126
canine units, 173, 208
*Carpathia*, 141
Centers for Disease Control and
    Prevention (CDC), 201
Chartier, William (Bill), 104–105, 198
Chelsea Piers, 140–141, 146, 156, 178,
    179–180
Chelsea Piers Sports and Entertainment
    Complex, 141
*Chelsea Screamer*, 97–100, 111, 166–167,
    178, 192, 195
children, 100, 132–133, 206–207. *see also*
    Silverton, Kate (Kitten)
Circle Line, 142–143, 145, 153, 167
Coast Guard, responsibilities of, 82, 120

Coast Guard Recruiting and Services
    Center, 209–210
Code of Federal Regulations (CFRs), 34,
    82, 120
Colgate Clock, 173, 217
Colicchio, Tom, 193
collaboration, drills on, 32
communications, 38–39, 108–109, 117–
    118, 160
Conlon, Paul, 62
containerization, 34–36, 129, 179
Cove to Cove race, 70
Coyle, John, 170–171
Crane, Dr. Michael, 201–202
currents, danger of, 45, 69–70, 83

Day, Michael, 88–89, 90–92, 114–115,
    118–120, 160–162, 164–166, 174, 180,
    184, 185, 212, 214
deaths. *see also* bodies, falling/jumping
    due to exposure, 200, 201
    official count of, 201–202
debris, removal of, 196
decontamination, 158
DonJon Marine, 187, 196
Dorhn, Glenn, 129–130, 132–133
Doswell, John, 148, 180, 200, 215
Dowling, Robert, 69
Downtown Boathouse, 134
Dunkirk evacuation, 7
Dunn-Jones, Felicia, 201
dust
    contents of, 56
    deaths and illness due to, 199–202, 207
    toxicity of, 152, 199

elevators, lack of operation of, 17–18
emergency preparedness, 81–82
Esposito, Joseph, 18, 28
*Excalibur*, 27, 136–139, 151, 175–176

F-15 Eagles, 19, 107
FDNY's Center for Terrorism and
    Disaster Preparedness, 204
Feal, John, 200
FealGood Foundation, 200
Federal Aviation Administration (FAA),
    19

ferries
    history of, 86–87
    ridership of, 188–189
fifteenth anniversary commemoration,
    3–4
*Fire Fighter II*, 204
fireboats, description of, 6
fireproofing material, 49
fires, effect of, 49–50
Flay, Bobby, 193
fleet expansion, 204–205
Flicker, Perry (Flick), 193–194
Flight 11
    commemoration of, 4
    FAA and, 19
    hijacking of, 19
    impact of, 10, 15, 16, 22
    notification of impact of, 11
    transmission from, 19
Flight 77, impact of, 47
Flight 175
    commemoration of, 4
    Flight 11 transmission and, 19
    impact of, 31, 37–38
*41497*, 32, 117, 190
Fox, Florence, 100–103, 105–106, 168–170,
    175, 206–207
*Frank Sinatra*, 14, 79
*Franklin Reinauer*, 130–131
Freitas, Greg, 98–99, 166, 178–179, 195
Fulton, Robert, 86, 127

Ganci, Peter, 64
Gately, Kevin, 87–88
General Store, The, 195
*George Washington*, 79, 82, 84, 141
Giants Stadium, 146
Gill, Huntley, 120–122, 178–179
Gillman, Billy, 37, 38, 93
Giuliani, Rudolph, 87, 115
Graceffo, Vince, 181
Grandinetti, Jerry, 26–27, 59–60, 61,
    136–139, 150, 151, 174, 175–176
Ground Zero, 6, 153, 174, 180, 192, 196,
    200–202, 206, 218

Hammitt, Josh, 28–29, 150
Hanchrow, Greg, 46, 47–48, 139–140,
    141–142, 143–144, 174, 176–177,
    180–184, 191–193
*Harbor Charlie*, 103, 208
Harbor Operations Committee, 165, 197,
    212–213
Harbor Operations Maritime Evacuation
    Subcommittee, 213
Harris, Patrick (deputy commander),
    11–12, 31, 88–89, 119, 162–164,
    165–166, 190, 215

Harris, Patrick (on *Ventura*), 9–11, 28–29,
    60–61, 145, 149–154, 194–195
Hayden, Peter, 17
Hayes, Timothy, 28
*Hayward*, 125–126
Haywood, Bob, Jr., 138
Haywood, Bob, Sr., 139, 151
helicopter rescue, impossibility of, 27–28
Henley, William Ernest, 4–5
*Henry Hudson*, 43, 44–45, 80
Hepburn, Alice, 154–156
Hepburn, Pamela, 154–155, 156–158
*Hercules*, 128
Holland Tunnel, 75
Homeland Security Act (2002), 210
*Horizon*, 147
*Houston Express*, 216
Hudson
    currents in, 45, 69–70
    tides in, 57
Hudson and Manhattan (H&M)
    Railroad/H&M Hudson Tubes, 75

*Ideal-X*, 34
illness due to exposure, 199–202
Imperatore, Arthur, Jr., 188–189
Imperatore, Arthur, Sr., 87, 217
infrastructure, rebuilding of, 189–190
International Naval Review and
    Operation Sail (OpSail) event,
    91–92, 119, 187
*Intrepid*, 167
Ivory, Tim, 121, 125–126, 178

*Janice Anne Reinauer*, 130
*Jersey*, 86
Johansen, Peter, 15, 50–51, 84, 135
*John D. McKean*, 36–39, 55, 57–58, 63,
    65–66, 93–96, 109–113, 122–124,
    126, 172–173, 174, 203, 205
*John J. Harvey*, 5–6, 120–122, 124–127,
    178, 180, 219
*John Reinauer*, 130

K-9 Units, 208
Kendra, James, 54, 162, 163
Kennedy, Sean, 97–100, 111, 166–167,
    178–179, 192, 195
Koenig, Fritz, 12
Krevey, Angela, 149, 155
Krevey, John, 146–148, 152, 156, 215
Kunz, Gray, 193

Lacey, Karen, 48–49, 67–69, 92–96, 109,
    111, 112–113, 167–168, 205–206
LaPlaca, Gina, 24–26, 77–79, 170–171
Larrabee, Richard, 72–74, 76, 184–186, 215
*Launch 9*, 104

*Lexington*, 27, 136
Liberty Island, 211
Liberty Park, 209
Liloia, Donald, 14, 15
Lincoln Harbor, 145, 153–154
Lincoln Harbor Yacht Club, 142, 145, 174
Long Slip, 157
*Lusitania*, 141

Manhattan
    demographics of, 20
    early ferry service for, 86
    number of people in, 20
    swimming around, 69–70
Manhattan Kayak Company, 149
man-overboard drills, 82
marine assistance, codification of, 54
Marine One, 36, 38
*Mariner III*, 178, 195
Maritime Security Level, 210
Marriott Hotel, 62, 72, 76
mass casualty incident (MCI) protocols, 108
McGovern, Andrew, 89, 91, 165–166, 182
McPhillips, Michael, 13–15, 79, 81, 82–84, 92, 141–142, 160, 192, 199–200, 202
McSwiggins Pub, 172
Metcalf, Ed, 36–37, 38, 40
Metropolitan Transportation Authority (MTA), 20–21
Meyer, Danny, 193
Miano, Dennis, 139, 144, 149, 151–154
*Mis Moondance*, 3
*Morgan Reinauer*, 130, 132–133

National Guardsmen, 178
*New York*, 91, 92, 114–115, 118, 119, 160, 164, 166, 174, 182
New York Circle Line Sightseeing Yachts, 142–143, 145, 153
New York City Department of Transportation (DOT), 20
New York harbor
    data on, 8–9
    size of, 9
    New York Waterway, 13–15, 87–88, 187–188
9/11 Maritime Medal, 200
9/11 Tribute Center, 205
*North River*, 127
North Tower
    collapse of, 97–98, 111, 134
    fireball in, 22
    first impact to, 10, 15, 16–17, 22
Northeast Air Defense Sector (NEADS), 19
Nussberger, Bob, 61–63, 71–72, 202–203
NYPD Harbor Unit, 208

NYPD's Emergency Service Unit (ESU), 18

Office of Emergency Management, 88, 174, 187, 195
O'Hara, Gene, 181–184, 192
Oldmixon, John, 90
OpSail event, 91–92, 119, 187
overcrowding
    concerns over, 88–89
    reporting of, 161

Palmer, Charlie, 193
*Paradise Built in Hell, A* (Solnit), 219–220
Parese, James, 55, 129, 171, 211
Parga, Gulmar, 36–37, 39–40, 55–57, 58, 93, 95–96, 111, 112
PATH (Port Authority Trans-Hudson Corporation) trains, 14, 20, 21, 75, 188
Pentagon, 66, 80
Perez, Carlos, 32–33, 51–52, 117–118, 174, 189, 190, 198
Petersen Boat Yard & Marina, 48, 139, 177
Peterson, Ken, 130–131, 133, 196–197
Pfeifer, Joseph, 16–17, 204
Phillips, Mark, 139, 194
Pier 11, 84
Pier 63 Maritime, 147–149, 152–153, 156, 194
Pintabona, Don, 193
Port Authority of New York and New Jersey
    closing of, 35
    containerization and, 34–35
    oversight from, 20
*Port Imperial*, 87
Port of New York and New Jersey
    cost of shutdown of, 186
    reopening of, 191
Ports, Waterways, and Coastal Security (PWCS), 210
Post, Kenneth "Bob," 33–34, 36
Powell, Tyrone, 104–105
*Powhatan*, 196
"Praise the Lord and Pass the Ammunition," 194–195
Preece, Jean, 180

radios, 38–39
Rear Admiral Richard E. Bennis Award, 215
Reetz, Chris, 115–117, 156–158, 172
Reinauer Transportation, 129–130, 144
rescue, compulsion to, 54
Responder Program, 201
Rockefeller, David, 74–75
Rokosz, Greg, 142, 145, 146, 174
Ronan, Daniel, 34, 35, 91, 186

Rooney, Bethann, 185, 212–214
Rosenkrantz, Bruce, 148, 155, 156
Ross, Robert, 211–212
*Royal Princess*, 27, 136, 149, 151–154, 194
rules, breaking of, 161–162
rumors, 110
Rumsfeld, Donald, 110
Ruthie's, 180
Ryan, Chris, 115–117, 156–158, 172

*Samuel I. Newhouse*, 55, 210–211
Sandy Hook Pilots, 35, 89–91, 119, 164, 165, 174, 216
Sasso, Frank, 158
Scarnecchia, Daniel, 143
SeaStreak, 87
security, changes to, 185, 212–214
September 11 Memorial, 209
September 11th Families' Association, 205
Silverstin, Larry, 13
Silverton, Kate (Kitten), 100–103, 105–106, 168–170, 175, 206–207
Silverton, Susan, 101, 175
Sirvent, Tony, 103–105, 106–107, 181, 197–198, 208
Slattery, Mickie, 109
Solnit, Rebecca, 219
South Tower
    collapse of, 51–52, 55–56, 59, 62, 64, 66, 67, 77, 80, 116, 149
    first impact to, 31, 37–38
"Sphere," 209
Spirit Cruises, 46, 139, 141–142, 143–145, 146, 153, 176–177, 181–184
*Spirit of America*, 217
*Spirit of New Jersey*, 140, 143–144, 184
*Spirit of New York*, 140, 143, 176–177, 181, 184, 191–193
*Spirit of the Hudson*, 140, 143, 184
St. Joseph's Chapel (St. Joe's Supply), 4–5, 193–194
Staten Island Ferry, 8, 87, 171, 189, 210–211, 216
Steamboat Act (1852), 82
steamboats, 86, 127–128
*Stephen Scott Reinauer*, 129
Suhr, Danny, 62
Sullivan, Tom, 40, 63–65, 112, 113, 123–124, 203–204, 205
Summers, Kenneth, 22, 37–38, 109
supplies, 174, 179–180, 192–193, 195–196
Survivor Program, 201

Thornton, Rick, 43–46, 80–81
*Three Forty-Three*, 204
*Titanic*, 54, 140–141
transportation shutdowns, 46–47, 52, 116, 149
triage centers, 107–109, 158
tugs, 127, 128–129, 216. *see also* Reinauer Transportation
tunnels
    closing of, 47, 52, 116, 149
    effect of on commute, 75, 86–87
    H&M Railroad and, 75
    reopening of, 188, 191

Varela, Rich, 30–31, 41–43, 65–66, 95, 112–113, 123, 172–173, 203–204
Vazquez, Janer, 145–146
*Ventura*, 9, 60–61, 145, 149–151, 194
Vessel Traffic Service (VTS), 11, 33–34, 114
VIP Yacht Cruises, 26, 27

Wachtendorf, Tricia, 54, 162, 163
water rescues, 82–83
Weeks Marine, 187, 196
Whyte, Tom, 122–127
Wiggs, Katherine, 111, 207–208
Wiggs, Tammy, 12–13, 48–49, 67–69, 70, 92–95, 109, 111–112, 167–168, 207–208
Wilson, Jaime, 119
Winter Garden, 28, 68, 97, 200
Woods, Greg, 93–94, 95–96
World Financial Center terminal, 84
World Trade Center. *see also* North Tower; South Tower
    bombing of, 17–18, 44
    building upgrades to, 74
    development of, 74–75
World Trade Center Health Program (WTCHP), 200–201, 202

Yamasaki, Minoru, 12, 73

Zadroga 9/11 Health and Compensation Act, James L., 200, 201
Zodiac, 59–60, 61
Zuccotti Park, 26

CPSIA information can be obtained
at www.ICGtesting.com
Printed in the USA
LVHW041043220723
753082LV00003B/278

9 781501 759123